Cambridge Elements ☰

Elements in Musical Theatre
edited by
William A. Everett
University of Missouri-Kansas City

A HUGE REVOLUTION OF THEATRICAL COMMERCE

Walter Mocchi and the Italian Musical Theatre Business in South America

Matteo Paoletti
University of Genoa

T0349760

CAMBRIDGE
UNIVERSITY PRESS

CAMBRIDGE
UNIVERSITY PRESS

University Printing House, Cambridge CB2 8BS, United Kingdom

One Liberty Plaza, 20th Floor, New York, NY 10006, USA

477 Williamstown Road, Port Melbourne, VIC 3207, Australia

314–321, 3rd Floor, Plot 3, Splendor Forum, Jasola District Centre,
New Delhi – 110025, India

79 Anson Road, #06–04/06, Singapore 079906

Cambridge University Press is part of the University of Cambridge.

It furthers the University's mission by disseminating knowledge in the pursuit of
education, learning, and research at the highest international levels of excellence.

www.cambridge.org
Information on this title: www.cambridge.org/9781108790482
DOI: 10.1017/9781108855990

First published 2020

A catalogue record for this publication is available from the British Library.

ISBN 978-1-108-79048-2 Paperback
ISSN 2631-6528 (online)
ISSN 2631-651X (print)

A Huge Revolution of Theatrical Commerce

Walter Mocchi and the Italian Musical Theatre Business in South America

Elements in Musical Theatre

DOI: 10.1017/9781108855990
First published online: July 2020

Matteo Paoletti
University of Genoa

Author for correspondence: Matteo Paoletti, matteo.paoletti@unige.it

Abstract: In the first third of the twentieth century, South America became the most important market for many European theatrical companies. When Italy found itself in various theatrical crises, Walter Mocchi created a transoceanic theatrical empire, using his business acumen to craft viable solutions. While his efforts were most visible in the sphere of opera, he played an extremely significant role in the promotion and circulation of popular forms of musical theatre (e.g. operetta) and staged world premieres of works by Italian superstars in Argentina (e.g. Mascagni's *Isabeau*), thus offering an early example of what Stephen Greenblatt calls 'cultural mobility'.

Keywords: theatre, Walter Mocchi, Pietro Mascagni, opera, operetta

ISBNs: 9781108790482 (PB), 9781108855990 (OC)
ISSNs: 2631-6528 (online), 2631-651X (print)

Contents

Introduction

From the 1890s until the mid-1920s, South America became the most important market for a large number of European theatrical companies. When competition from operetta and cinema created a financial crisis for opera and spoken theatre companies at the dawn of the twentieth century, visionary impresarios took these companies from Italy, France, and Spain to the major cities of Argentina, Uruguay, and Brazil. As part of the entertainment industry's first stage of globalization, European companies discovered in the New World a growing theatrical marketplace with weak copyright laws, lower operating costs, and an increasing thirst for cultural consumption. A handful of Italian impresarios held this South American market firmly under their collective control. As pointed out by P. B. Gheusi, manager of the Opéra Comique in Paris: 'Italians are indeed, in contemporary music, what the Genoese were on the seas in the feudal times. They hold the keys of the world market in the universal theatrical business.'[1]

The most important of these impresarios was Walter Mocchi (b.1871, Turin; d.1955, Rio de Janeiro), a journalist and socialist revolutionary who entered the business of opera after marrying the noted soprano Emma Carelli (b.1877, Naples; d.1928, Montefiascone). Mocchi's career lasted for nearly half a century, and his successes in Italy, France, Spain, Brazil, and Argentina made him an exemplary paradigm of an interoceanic impresario.[2] After serving as an artillery lieutenant in Turin, in 1892 he left the army to study law in Naples, where he quickly rose to fame as a brilliant politician and orator in the local socialist party. In 1897 he took part in the famous revolutionary expedition to Greece led by the anarchist Amilcare Cipriani. After returning to Naples, Mocchi worked as a journalist for the socialist newspaper *Avanti!* (Forward!) and in 1898 he organized the *moti partenopei* (risings of Naples), the events of which he described in a memoir.[3]

That same year he married Emma Carelli, who in 1899 received critical and popular acclaim for her performances at two of Italy's leading opera houses, the Costanzi in Rome and the Teatro alla Scala in Milan. Carelli remained especially renowned for her performances in verismo and Puccini roles, and Mocchi

---

[1] P. B. Gheusi, *Guerre et Théâtre* (Berger-Levrault, 1919), p. 316. All translations from French, Italian, German, Spanish and Portuguese are by the author.

[2] Mocchi's political life has been well documented (for an overview see: A. Cimmino, 'Walter Mocchi', in *Dizionario Biografico degli Italiani* (Istituto dell'Enciclopedia italiana, 1960–), vol. 75 (2011)). However, for a long time his theatrical activity was known because of his harsh judgements concerning Arturo Toscanini, Titta Ruffo, Gino Marinuzzi, and Pietro Mascagni. These artists all described the impresario in negative terms, which affected his legacy and reputation. If Mocchi the man was indeed unprincipled and shady, his importance in the development and exploitation of the theatrical market is unquestionable.

[3] W. Mocchi, *I moti italiani del 1898: lo stato d'assedio a Napoli e le sue conseguenze* (Enrico Muca, 1901).

supported her career while simultaneously pursuing his political connections. As reported by the secret police, who always remained attentive to the activities of those of left-wing sympathies, during Carelli's 1902 South American tour her husband sponsored revolutionary-themed lectures in Buenos Aires. While she was performing at the Opera in Buenos Aires, Mocchi engaged in typical theatricalism when he employed a group of political anarchists to serve 'as an enthusiast and zealous claque, which one night, with total American exaggeration, after the show removed the horses from Carelli's carriage and pulled her coach to the hotel'.[4]

After returning to Italy, the couple moved to Milan, where Mocchi became the theorist of the revolutionary fringe of the socialist party. In 1904 he was among the leaders of the general strike that paralysed the entire country and brought about a series of new elections. Mocchi's political activism caused problems for his wife's career, for after the 1904 general strike, the main theatres and publishers in Italy would no longer engage her. Carelli's resulting suicide attempt caused a huge press sensation and a few months later, after Mocchi lost an election campaign for the Italian parliament, he quit politics to become his wife's agent. His appearance on the theatrical market stage, like his political activism, was sudden and disruptive.

In 1907, in partnership with some of the most important figures in the Argentine business community, Mocchi established the Sociedad Teatral Ítalo-Argentina (STIA) in Buenos Aires. This was a joint-stock company with a large share capital, whose purpose was to create a trust among the most important South American theatres. The company aimed to tackle the crisis that was consuming the operatic world at the time by renewing the system of production, following the financial and managerial models of the emerging US theatre industry. The press defined the STIA as 'a huge revolution of theatrical commerce.'[5] In a very short time, the enterprise had gained control of the main opera houses in Argentina, Chile, Brazil, and Uruguay (among them, the Colón and the Coliseo in Buenos Aires and the 'Municipals' in Rio, Santiago, and São Paulo), as well as some prominent spoken-drama theatres (i.e. the Avenida and the Odeón, which specialized in the Spanish and the French repertoires, but also staged opera and operetta). For its activities, the STIA engaged the most important companies from Europe (including those led by Charles le Bargy, Lugné-Poe, Suzanne Desprès, Ermete Novelli, Emma Gramatica, Giulio Marchetti, Emilio Sagi-Barba, and Scognamiglio–Caramba), leading composers (such as Pietro Mascagni and Luigi Dall'Argine), conductors (including

---

[4] ACS, *CPC*, b. 3321, Police report to the Minister of the Interior, Buenos Aires, 16 September 1902.

[5] 'S.T.I.A.–S.T.I.N.', *Il Teatro Illustrato*, 5 November 1908.

Hector Panizza and Luigi Mancinelli) and – of course – singing stars (for example, Titta Ruffo, Gilda Dalla Rizza, Emma Carelli, and Maria Farneti).

In 1908 Mocchi created a similar enterprise in Italy by establishing the Società Teatrale Internazionale (STIN) in partnership with the publisher Edoardo Sonzogno, Teatro alla Scala manager Uberto Visconti di Modrone, and other prominent members of the Italian theatrical community. During its first season, the STIN purchased the Teatro Costanzi, the most important opera house in Rome, and soon thereafter was in control of some of the most important theatres in Italy. The interoceanic trust meant that artists engaged by the STIN and STIA could perform all year long and take full advantage of the comple-mentary theatrical season schedules between the two hemispheres. Once the Italian season ended, the productions would travel to South America, where they would perform during the southern hemisphere's winter season. The STIN struggled throughout its existence and was ultimately unsuccessful, despite its high-profile proposed ventures (including the Italian premiere of Debussy's *Pelléas et Mélisande*).

On the other side of the Atlantic, however, Mocchi flourished. Through a new company he established in 1910 to take over the operations of STIA, La Teatral, the impresario organized tours of Sonzogno's new productions as well as offering the world premiere of Mascagni's *Isabeau*, *Il piccolo Marat*, and other new operas by lesser-known composers, such as Gian Francesco Malipiero's *Canossa* and Gino Marinuzzi's *Jacquerie*.

Mocchi developed an extensive theatrical network on both sides of the Atlantic that included theatres, other impresarios and managers, music publish-ers, production companies, and star singers. This level of integration extends to the repertory he produced in both Italy and South America. Operas, spoken plays, and operettas all appeared on Mocchi's stages, and these genres were inextricably linked in terms of Mocchi's entrepreneurial vision. In order to understand the role of operetta in Mocchi's enterprise, it must be viewed in tandem with other theatrical genres.

Operetta held a special place in Mocchi's empire. Realizing that money would be lost when mounting opera and spoken plays, Mocchi included operetta performances in his seasons as a way to balance the budget and offset the costs of operas and plays through ticket sales. He knew that operettas had greater audience appeal and therefore sold better than his other offerings. Mocchi thus 'absorbed in his capitalistic vortex'[6] the operetta companies of Giulio Marchetti (born Mario Ascoli, 1858–1916) and Caramba (stage name of Luigi Sapelli,

---

[6] 'La Compagnia della "Teatral" diretta da Marchetti parte per Buenos Aires', *Il Teatro Illustrato*, 1–15 February, 1910.

1865–1936), the latter the famed costume designer at La Scala[7] who held the Italian rights to Lehár's *The Merry Widow*, among other works.[8] Despite the vibrant zarzuela tradition that existed throughout South America at the time,[9] this genre never figured into Mocchi's Eurocentric enterprise.

Mocchi's wide-ranging theatrical interests served him well during World War I and the years that followed. During World War I, with the support of the French and Italian governments, the impresario organized a 'combination' that included La Scala, Costanzi, Colón, L'Opéra (Paris), and Opéra Comique (Paris) and kept these major opera houses on both sides of the Atlantic open during wartime.

In 1922 and 1923, Mocchi fulfilled a new demand among Argentine audiences for Wagnerian *Musikdrama* by organizing South American tours of the Vienna Philharmonic conducted by Felix Weingartner (1922) and Richard Strauss (1923). While these tours had the distinction of offering for the first time the original versions of Wagner's operas in South America, they also generated a great deal of criticism. Mascagni, who participated in Mocchi's 1922 tour but was overshadowed by Weingartner, denounced his former ally to the fascists as the 'Buffalo Bill of the Italian impresarios abroad', who 'offends the Italian art by preferring German artists and repertoire'.[10] The powerful Mocchi, who supported Mussolini, managed to turn this personal controversy into a large-scale debate that played out in the press. This confrontation caused a crisis in musical theatre in terms of repertory, distribution, and funding. This heated dialogue in turn led to two important congresses: the Conference for the Lyrical Theatre that took place in Rome in 1923 and the Conference for the Dramatic and Operetta Theatre organized in Milan the following year. During these meetings, leading industry figures were forced to recognize that the 'crisis of the musical theatre [wa]s a partial aspect of a more general crisis, because it [wa]s not a mere economic crisis: it [wa]s a cultural crisis'.[11] As a result of the discussions, the Italian fascist state (which was in power from 1922 through 1943) intervened and enacted reforms in the performing arts.

In the late 1920s Mocchi moved to Brazil, where after the death of his first wife he married the rising opera star Bidu Sayão (born Balduína de Oliveira Sayão,

---

[7]   V. Crespi Morbio (ed.), *Caramba: mago del costume* (Amici della Scala, 2008).

[8]   For a general overview of operetta and its reception in Italy, see: P. Nugnes and S. Massimini, *Storia dell'Operetta* (Ricordi, 1984); W. Fiorentino, *L'operetta italiana: storia, analisi critica, aneddoti* (Catinaccio, 2006).

[9]   For information on zarzuela at the time, see K. McCleary, 'Mass, Popular, and Elite Culture? The Spanish Zarzuela in Buenos Aires, 1890–1900', *Studies in Latin American Popular Culture*, 21 (2002), 1–27.

[10] 'Mascagni e Walter Mocchi alle mani', *La Stampa*, 15 March 1923.

[11] 'I voti del Congresso per il Teatro lirico', *Il Popolo d'Italia*, 16 March 1923.

1902–1999). He remained connected to Italian politics and returned to his homeland in the 1930s, where, as a supporter of the fascist state, he became involved
with the movie and radio industries. After World War II, Mocchi moved back to
Brazil, where he kept his hand in the various aspects of the nation's theatrical
sphere until his death in 1955.

Mocchi's theatrical career provides a revealing case study of a major impresario working in both Europe and South America who produced different types
of theatre, including opera, spoken-word plays, and operetta. If we study the
companies he established, the artistic projects he produced, the interrelation-
ships between these various endeavours and his tight relationship with the
publisher Sonzogno and the composer Mascagni, it becomes clear that the
production of musical theatre in the early twentieth century was a truly commercial enterprise with clear aspects of vertical integration, transatlantic networks, and marketplace realities.[12]

1. Crisis in Italy, Opportunity in South America: Theatrical Economies at the Turn of the Twentieth Century

As the twentieth century took hold in Italy, music publishers largely controlled
the repertory that appeared on stages, pushing aside the traditional impresarios
of the previous generation. This fundamental economic shift was part of the so-
called 'Giolitti era'" (named for Giovanni Giolitti, the prime minister at the
time), or liberal 'take-off.' Between 1897 and 1914, Italy's society and economy
underwent tremendous growth. During these years the gross domestic product
grew from 12 to 19 billion lire, and the gross national income increased from
60,139 to 90,033 million lire.[13] Italy – or more precisely some areas of it, mostly
in the north – quickly developed from a largely agricultural country to an
industrial power.

The power of the publishers resulted from the crisis that emerged as theatre
developed into an entertainment industry[14] and opera lost its 'mythical monopoly' over other genres.[15] Audience tastes and demands were changing, and the
operatic establishment suffered increasing competition from lighter stage genres (including operetta) and cinema. Old-style independent impresarios who
selected repertoire, commissioned new works, hired singers, and secured

---

[12] On the role of theatrical agents in the transatlantic trade see: N. Leonhardt, *Theater über Ozeane: Vermittler transatlantischen Austauschs (1890–1925)* (Vandenhoeck & Ruprecht, 2018).

[13] G. Barone, 'La modernizzazione italiana dalla crisi allo sviluppo', in G. Sabbatucci and V. Vidotto (eds.), *Storia d'Italia* (Laterza, 1995), vol. III, pp. 256–370.

[14] C. Sorba. 'The Origins of the Entertainment Industry: The Operetta in Late Nineteenth-Century Italy', *Journal of Modern Italian Studies*, 2 (2006), 282–302.

[15] G. Salvetti, 'Dal Verdi della maturità a Giacomo Puccini', in A. Basso (ed.), *Musica in scena – Storia dello spettacolo musicale* (Utet, 1996), p. 403.

venues were finding themselves unable to reinvent their long-standing practices.[16] To minimize losses, these impresarios ended up planning their seasons around an increasingly smaller number of familiar titles from the past. Opera impresarios were considered to be unreliable individuals who were always on the verge of bankruptcy and who could hardly ever rely on public funding to finance their productions.[17] Theatrical grants from municipalities, a mainstay of the arts economy, had been declared 'discretionary' in Italy in 1867, and until 1936, municipalities could choose whether to support operatic activity with a *dote* (grant) or to leave their opera houses closed. The latter often happened, even in major cities.[18] Usually only lyrical (operatic) seasons could be sure of receiving grants, thus making opera the only non-commercial genre to require such financial support for its very survival.

To continue its existence, opera, like its cousin operetta, had to become a commercial genre. Although opera still represented an exclusive rite for upper-class society and had become increasingly popular with the middle class,[19] audiences often preferred boulevard or operetta theatres rather than opera houses. 'The new rich have chosen another kind of amusement', stated the theatre manager Franco Liberati: 'they go where they feel welcomed better, where they understand more easily, where they get bored less.'[20]

In order to keep their operas before the public in this changing environment, music publishers became producers. They firmly controlled the repertoire and the entire production and distribution channels for nearly all operas and spoken theatrical performances.[21] They purchased translation rights to the most successful foreign plays, commissioned new scores from their own librettists and composers, distributed their operas to carefully chosen theatres, and controlled the staging of their properties through the required rental of costumes, sceneries, props, and exclusive contracts for conductors and *direttori di scena* (stage directors).

While new publishers specializing in operetta (e.g. Suvini Zerboni) conquered large market shares and started to run their own theatres,[22] the historical

---

[16] C. Sorba, "To Please the Public: Composers and Audiences in Nineteenth-Century in Italy," *Journal of Interdisciplinary History*, 36 (2006), 595–614.

[17] J. Rosselli, *The Opera Industry in Italy from Cimarosa to Verdi: The Role of the Impresario* (Cambridge University Press, 1984).

[18] I. Piazzoni, "Il governo e la politica per il teatro: tra promozione e censura (1882–1900)," in C. Sorba (ed.), *L'Italia fin de siècle a teatro* (Carocci, 2004), pp. 61–100.

[19] F. Nicolodi, "Il teatro lirico e il suo pubblico," in S. Soldani and G. Turi (eds.), *Fare gli italiani* (Il Mulino, 1993), vol. I, pp. 257–339.

[20] "I risultati del Congresso dei Lirici esposti alla 'Stampa' da un competente," *La Stampa*, 17 March 1923.

[21] S. Baia Curioni, *Mercanti dell'Opera: Storie di Casa Ricordi* (Il Saggiatore, 2011), p. 181.

[22] Sonzogno also developed his entrepreneurial activities, mostly in the Teatro Lirico of Milan, where he staged the main verismo operas and where Enrico Caruso debuted with *Arlesiana* (1897). M. Capra, 'La Casa Editrice Sonzogno tra giornalismo e impresariato', in M. Morini and

market leaders Ricordi and Sonzogno produced a huge number of new operas to meet the changing tastes of the audience. Between 1900 and 1915, 250 new titles were launched in Italy, although most of them were destined to run for just a few performances and were quickly forgotten.[23] Very few living composers managed to find space on the marquees: 'people are wary of a new that has not satisfied them too many times and for which they feel no transport,' asserted one writer.[24] The taste of the audience and the evolution of musical style in Italy, however, had never been that far apart.

The efforts of the music publishing industry in terms of printing and producing opera were immense. In 1902 the *Nuovo Gran Catalogo Ricordi* listed more than 100,000 imprints, including sheet music and scores.[25] Two years later, the Sonzogno catalogue boasted 112 Italian and 55 French operas.[26] While the publishers did their best to fill houses, the lack of audience was having a serious impact on the finances of the Italian theatre industry. A new market was essential, and a quickly developing one lay across the Atlantic Ocean in South America.

At the turn of the twentieth century, relentless growth was taking place in South America; its most advanced areas could now compete with Europe and the United States in terms of wealth and cultural demand. In Argentina the expansion of railways into many areas of the country that were agriculturally fertile meant that 'unemployment almost disappeared, even though the distribution of wealth remained unequal.'[27] Massive levels of migration from Europe was needed for this explosion of activity. In the early 1900s, immigration to South American from Italy reached impressive numbers: between 1901 and 1910, Italian authorities recorded 602,669 expats living in South America, and from 1901 to 1915, 1,126,513 Sicilians left Italy for the New World.[28] The exodus was sustained by European governments as part of a strategy that 'conceived emigration in terms of political hegemony', and Italy's leaders aimed to make of Argentina 'a new and greater Italy ... for mercantile and industrial expansionism'.[29]

P.Ostali Jr. (eds.), *Casa Musicale Sonzogno: Cronologie, saggi, testimonianze* (Sonzogno, 1995), vol. I, pp. 243–290.

[23] R. Zanetti, *La musica italiana nel Novecento*, 3 vols. (Bramante, 1985), vol. I, pp. 53–99.

[24] 'L'opera nuova del maestro Franco Alfano', *Corriere Mercantile*, 4 February 1909.

[25] F. Degrada, 'Il segno e il suono: storia di un editore musicale e del suo mondo', in *Musica, musicisti, editoria: 175 anni di Casa Ricordi, 1808–1983* (Ricordi, 1983), pp. 22–3.

[26] M. Morini and P. Ostali, Jr., 'Cronologia della Casa Musicale Sonzogno', in *Casa Musicale Sonzogno ...*, vol. I, p. 345.

[27] B. Seibel, *Historia del teatro argentino: Desde los rituales hasta 1930* (Corregidor, 2002), p. 381.

[28] P. Audenino and P. Corti, *L'emigrazione italiana* (La Fenice 2000, 1994), pp. 20–1.

[29] E. Gentile, 'L'emigrazione italiana in Argentina nella politica di espansione del nazionalismo e del Fascismo', *Storia contemporanea*, 3 (1986), 357.

Cultural consumption grew alongside this commercial development, which meant that the rise of theatrical and musical production in South America was strongly connected to economic development and migration dynamics. Buenos Aires became a cultural as well as political capital and earned itself the moniker of the 'Paris of South America'.[30] In 1905 Buenos Aires was a multicultural metropolis with 1.3 million inhabitants, and 2.6 million tickets were sold for its theatres in that one year. The number of spectators that year was twice the city's population. The number of theatregoers had doubled by 1907, when 4.2 million people attended, 600,000 of which were cinemagoers. Theatre was one way for immigrant communities to stay connected to their homelands, and it thrived for this reason.[31] Buenos Aires theatres catered to a wide range of tastes and prices. Some specialized in national repertoires (e.g. the Odeón, patronized by the French community, usually engaged companies coming from France), while others offered typical Argentine genres such as *sainete criollo* or the ever-popular zarzuela. These works typically included immigrant characters,[32] often Italians.[33] Opera, though, became the leading genre and played on several stages, from those featuring non-professional troupes to the glamorous Teatro Colón.

The splendidly refurbished Teatro Colón offered a visual representation of the rising commercial bourgeoisie that ruled Argentina's economic growth. On its reopening in 1908, the press hailed it as 'el más grande y hermoso de los de Sud América, y uno de los principales del mundo' (the largest and most beautiful of those [theatres] in South America, and one of the main ones of the world),[34] while magazines published the names of the families that could afford season tickets, divided per tier, according to the old practice of buying a box to be watched, rather than to watch. In venues such as the Colón, the new upper class was constructing its own identity by imitating Europeans in brand-new opera houses designed in lavish classical Italian styles, with tiers of boxes surmounted by galleries. South America, therefore, had both audiences that craved Italian opera and new theatres in which it could be performed.

---

[30] C. E. Benzecry, An Opera House for the 'Paris of South America': Pathways to the Institutionalization of High Culture', *Theory and Society*, 43 (2014), 169–96.

[31] F. J. Devoto, *Historia de la inmigración en la Argentina* (Editorial Sudamericana, 2003); F. J. Devoto and M.Madero (eds.), *Historia de la vida privada en la Argentina. La Argentina plural: 1870–1913* (Taurus, 2006, II), pp. 227–74.

[32] J. Rosselli, 'The Opera Business and the Italian Immigrant Community in Latin America 1820–1930: The Example of Buenos Aires', *Past & Present*, 127 (1990), 155–82; J. Rosselli, 'Latin America and Italian Opera: A Process of Interaction, 1810–1930', *Revista de musicologia*, 16 (1993), 139–45.

[33] O. Pellettieri (ed.), *Inmigración italiana y teatro argentino* (Galerna, 1999).

[34] 'Colón. Recuerdo temporada 1908', *La Revista Artística de Buenos Aires*, 30 August 1908.

With the theatrical crisis taking place in Italy, enterprising impresarios saw a tremendous opportunity to bring Italian companies to South America. European companies had been travelling to South America since the late eighteenth century, when they had performed familiar repertoire in precarious theatres for immigrant audiences.[35] Now, they staged new operas with sumptuous costumes and scenery carried from Europe, and extended their tours in terms of length and locations by travelling the inner rivers and establishing new theatres in more remote areas.

The scheme worked for several reasons. First, the South American theatrical seasons were complementary to the European ones. As the summer approached in Europe, winter – the traditional opera season – was on the horizon in South America. As the transatlantic shipping system became faster and more reliable, many artists and impresarios turned into 'commuters between Italy and South America',[36] as enthusiastically described in the Italian press:

> By now America has become an Italian colony, for what concerns theatre in general and especially for musical theatre. In a few years our art has had such success that our main impresarios compete for the best artists with fabulous prices. The lyrical seasons, at first a few and of slight importance, have multiplied in a 'Rossini crescendo' and they are nowadays real events. And as the Italian spring blooms, when our main opera houses close, the great liners welcome on board the best of what we had admired and applauded, sailing to North and South America.[37]

Furthermore, opera, with its foreign singers, conductors, and orchestral musicians, along with its increased ticket prices and size of productions, became a symbol of social prestige. Arturo Padovani, who managed the opera houses in Santiago de Chile and Valparaiso, noted: 'In 1906 the box seat auction [*remate*] raised 500,000 Escudos . . . . Ten years ago, for the same theatres we just needed an orchestra with twenty-six players . . . and a harmonium!'[38]

South American markets for Italian opera had become even healthier than the Italian one. The situation in Italy would only worsen. With the high demand for foreign singers on South American opera stages, opera stars demanded increased salaries, and companies in South America were able to pay. This

---

[35] A. E. Cetrangolo, *Ópera, barcos y banderas: El melodrama y la migración en Argentina (1880– 1920)* (Biblioteca Nueva, 2015).

[36] A. E. Cetrangolo, 'L'opera nei Paesi Latino-americani nell'età moderna e contemporanea', in A. Basso (ed.), *Musica in scena – Storia dello spettacolo musicale* (Utet, 1996), vol. 2, p. 669.

[37] 'Le compagnie liriche in America', *Il Teatro Illustrato*, 15–30 April 1907.   [38] Ibid.

Figure 1.1 Walter Mocchi in 1907 *(Il Teatro illustrato)*

situation had a negative impact on the Italian operatic scene, which could not match the fees paid overseas. As an example, Emma Carelli wrote to the manager of the Teatro Costanzi in Rome: 'If you think that it might be bad paying me L. 40,000 for the whole Carnival season, consider this: in America that is what I earn in a single month, and next year I will be paid 60,000. Respectful greetings, and I quit.'[39]

Companies also found advantages in South America due to the lack of copyright laws there. In Buenos Aires, the Sociedad de autores dramáticos y líricos (Society of Dramatic and Operatic Authors) was not established until 1907, and closed shortly thereafter due to conflicts among its members.[40] This meant that European companies could charge high ticket prices and still attract audiences, and also take advantage of royalty-free zones in order to add to their profits.

All in all, an unbalanced situation intensified the gulf between the Italian and the South American markets. Walter Mocchi (see Figure 1.1) summarized the situation in Italy thus: 'While the quantity of artists is decreasing . . . the number of theatres competing for them is increasing. This disproportion is the reason

---

[39] ASC, *STIN*, b. 4, fasc. 8, Telegram from Emma Carelli to Alberto Marghieri, 22 April 1909.
[40] Seibel, *Historia del teatro argentino*, p. 416.

why not only in Turin and Italy, but in all of Europe all the seasons are having problems.'[41] With this added to the fact that artists were demanding higher salaries because of what they could earn in South America, a true crisis had come about. Mocchi, while accompanying his wife, soprano Emma Carelli, on her South American tours, noticed the unevenness of practices between Italy and South America. Ever the forward-thinking entrepreneur, in 1905 he envisioned the creation of a large theatrical trust spanning Italy and South America that would break down competition, decrease costs through economies of scale, and force artists to lower their fees. Two years later he established the STIA, and transatlantic theatrical practices would be forever changed.

2. Mocchi in South America: The Sociedad Teatral Ítalo-Argentina

Of all the events concerning the South American theatrical market in the early twentieth century, none were more significant than the establishment of the Sociedad Teatral Ítalo-Argentina (STIA). The joint-stock company was founded in Buenos Aires on 23 September 1907, with a share capital of 3,000,000 pesos[42] (approximately €1.5 million in 2019)[43] for the purpose 'of exploiting the South American theatrical business in English and North American style'.[44] As its visionary founder Walter Mocchi stated, the STIA wanted 'to transform the market – which has been up to now a gamble of isolated and impecunious men – into an industry led by a strong capitalistic organization'.[45] Even though a joint-stock company could not be considered novel in either the European or US theatrical businesses at the time,[46] the legal form and aims of the STIA marked a clear difference between its form of corporate organization and the traditional role of impresarios. In a limited company, a board of directors representing the capital investors managed the company's affairs rather than a sole individual who represented himself. Although some theatrical collaborations had previously

---

[41] 'Un colloquio con Walter Mocchi sul programma della Società teatrale Internazionale', *La Stampa*, 20 February 1909.

[42] *Boletin Oficial de la República Argentina*, a. XV, n. 4212, 29 November 1907.

[43] The number is based on data provided by the Cámara Argentina de Casas y Agencias de Cambio (Argentine Chamber of Houses and Agencies of Change): www.cadecac.com.ar/historico01.php (accessed 2 October 2019).

[44] *La Revista Teatral de Buenos Aires*, 1 October 1907.

[45] 'La grande Società teatrale Italo Argentina', *Il Teatro Illustrato*, 15 November 1907.

[46] In 1898 the Teatro alla Scala was turned into a limited company, and by the turn of the century several sectors of the Italian market were dominated by the Suvini Zerboni or the Società Anonima Italiana Imprese Teatrali, the latter established in 1906 in Turin with 3,000,000 lire share capital.

existed in South America,[47] the sheer financial power of the STIA created a true theatrical trust. Its purpose was clear and direct:

> The new company aims to run as many theatres as possible, with the purpose not ... of creating a monopoly, but of ruling the local theatrical industry – both in lyric theatre and spoken drama and in operetta – with modern standards, by commercially erasing competition, which is often fatal, [and] replacing the risk of dubious exploitation with the certainty of constant benefits.[48]

While setting up his enterprise, Mocchi met Charles Séguin (1877–1930 see Figure 2.1), a French entrepreneur who had moved to Argentina when he was about eighteen and in a short time had become the head of a diversified economic empire.[49] Séguin was an influential shareholder of the Banco Francés del Rio de la Plata and provided Mocchi with the financial means to found the STIA, whose members included the most influential figures of the Argentine economic and political worlds.[50] The company attracted additional capital from small investors through a subscription campaign advertised in the press.

As a former journalist, Mocchi knew how to market his ideas. He wrote that an investment in the STIA would not only ensure 'a glorious economic advantage for the shareholders, but also a visible return for the audience ... by bringing to the theatres exclusively managed by the STIA ... the most renowned artists of the world, both in opera and in drama'.[51] Mocchi's charisma drew investors. In a further marketing effort, Mocchi also bought magazines (e. g. *Il Teatro illustrato* (The Illustrated Theatre), in partnership with Sonzogno) to

---

[47] Most significant was the arrangement in Buenos Aires between Cesare Ciacchi of the Teatro Politeama and Angelo Ferrari of the Teatro Colón. After many disagreements, in 1890 the two theatres started to organize their seasons together within a single large company. Ciacchi also had connections and underhanded agreements with his cousin, Luigi Ducci, an impresario in Chile, Brazil, Bolivia, and Peru, and Arturo Padovani, owner of the main theatres in Santiago de Chile. Ciacchi and Padovani played important roles in the STIA, and Ducci later became one of Mocchi's partners in La Teatral (M. Paoletti, 'La red de empresarios europeos en Buenos Aires (1880–1925). Algunas consideraciones preliminares', *Revista Argentina de Musicología*, 21 (2020), 51–76).

[48] 'La grande Società teatrale Italo Argentina.'

[49] Through his agency Tournée Séguin, established in Paris, Séguin organized South American tours for many European artists. They appeared in theatres and casinos Séguin built and owned in Argentina and Uruguay. Séguin controlled the Buenos Aires French-language newspaper *Le Courrier de la Plata*, and several mines and electric and construction companies. Some opponents, including the poet Enrique Cadícamo, suspected that Séguin's empire was built on connections with the underworld and prostitution (C. Szwarcer, *Teatro Maipo: 100 años de historia entre bambalinas* (Corregidor, 2010), pp. 25–6).

[50] Charles Séguin, as CEO, was chairman of the board, with the businessman César González Segura serving as president. Board members consisted of jurist and government consultant Antonio Tarnassi, journalist Andrés Luzio (founder of the *Corriere d'Italia*), Alejandro Olivero, León Forqués, Carlos Aubone, and Ángel Alegría. Mocchi was appointed 'General Agent for Europe'.

[51] 'Desarollo del comercio teatral en Buenos Aires', *Caras y Caretas*, 7 November 1908. The advertisement also contained a 'Boleto de suscripción' with which to order shares.

Figure 2.1 Charles Séguin in 1907 (*Il Teatro Illustrato*)

ensure the constant support of the press, and regularly financed editors and critics. He understood the importance of publicity.

Mocchi's next task was to establish an agency in Milan that could directly provide artists, musicians, and scores to South America while cutting brokerage costs.[52] This became the starting point for the establishment of an Italian branch of the STIA, which was founded on 24 July 1908, under the name the STIN. (The STIN is the focus of the next section.) Although the two companies were formally independent and each had different statutes and shareholders, they operated in a tight connection, along the lines of a twenty-first-century holding company.

The appearance of the STIA disrupted the South American theatrical economy. Shortly after its establishment, the enterprise was in control of the most important theatres in South America, including seven of the nine Category I theatres in Buenos Aires (Colón, Circo Arena, Coliseo, Odeón, Avenida, Costitución, Victoria), the Ópera and the Olimpo in Rosario, and several theatres in Chile, including the Socrates in Valparaíso and the 'Municipals' in Concepción, Santiago, and Talca. The STIA's holdings expanded the following year with the acquisition of the Solís in Montevideo (the capital of Uruguay), as

---

[52] The agency opened on 15 January 1908 with the purchase of the premises of the theatrical magazine *L'Arte Drammatica*.

well as the main theatres in the Brazilian cities of Rio de Janeiro and São Paulo. The STIA also procured smaller theatres, such as the Teatro Municipal of Santiago de Estero, located between Rosario and Tucumán in northern Argentina.[53]

The STIA was established through separate agreements with the impresarios who managed each venue. The agency itself took on all the financial risk. As each impresario transferred their theatres to the company, they became artistic directors without any fiscal responsibilities and were legally bound to hire their entire staff according to STIA agreements. This included not only artistic staff but also accountants, box-office employees, and the like. In exchange for their autonomy, impresarios received fixed wages, percentages of box-office receipts, and stock options.

With its aggressive policy, the STIA connected some of the key figures of theatrical commerce in South America.[54] The most important was probably Faustino da Rosa (1861–1936), owner of the main dramatic venues in Buenos Aires (the Odeón and the Avenida), who had in the past managed tours by the legendary Italian actress Eleonora Duse and the esteemed Spanish actress Maria Guerrero, the latter of whom eventually settled in Buenos Aires and became a producer herself.[55] Like his colleagues, da Rosa was concerned not only with the main opera houses but also sometimes with smaller venues. In 1908, thanks to a favourable agreement with the local government, da Rosa built at his own expense the Teatro y Casino in Tucumán, although the role of the STIA in this operation still remains unclear.[56]

Another crucial figure in the STIA was Cesare Ciacchi (1843–1913), owner of the Teatro Politeama and the acknowledged dean of theatrical commerce in Buenos Aires. In 1908 the municipality granted Ciacchi control of the newly refurbished Teatro Colón, which he then transferred to the STIA through an

---

[53] V. Demarzat, 'Le trust des Théâtres à Buenos-Ayres', *Comœdia*, 1 September 1909.

[54] In addition to those figures discussed here, others of significance included Luigi Carpentiero (Argentina), Arturo Padovani (Chile), and João Cateysson (Brazil).

[55] Faustino da Rosa was born in Lisbon in 1861, the son of impresario José Antonio da Rosa. After studying singing in Padua, he debuted as a bass in *Ernani* (Rovigo, 1899) but soon moved to Madrid and Argentina to start his entrepreneurial career. (S. Bastos, *Carteira do Artista: Apontamentos para a Historia do Theatro Portuguez e Brazileiro* (Bertrand, 1898), p. 382.) Da Rosa's partnership with Mocchi lasted beyond the STIA; in 1922 they jointly obtained a grant to run the Colón, and in 1923 they built and ran the Teatro Independencia in Mendoza.

[56] Da Rosa built a hotel, a casino, and a theatre, all of which he promised to keep open from April to September. In return, the Argentine government granted him a thirty-year concession, during which he would not have to pay taxes and would have to donate 15 per cent of his profits to charity or public education. Mocchi's name never appears in the official records. ('Ley n. 972, 18 August 1908', in Felin Linares Alurralde (ed.), *Compilación ordenada de leyes, decretos y mensajes del periodo constitucional de la Provincia de Tucumán: que comienza en la año 1852* (Imprenta de la Càrcel Penitenciaría, 1923), vol. XXXII, p. 130.)

underhanded agreement that, not surprisingly, caused tremendous controversy.[57] The Colón, as the premier opera house with public (municipal) funding, held a distinctive place within the STIA enterprise. Per the terms of the public grant, the municipality legally controlled artistic matters, a role the STIA sought to take over. It was indeed successful, and during the opening season even engaged a *régisseur* (Remo Ercolani) to supervise the staging, while its press advertisements made proud mention of its Viennese and Italian suppliers of scenery, costumes, and props, adding to the prestige of their productions.

The STIA's theatres created a network for the circulation of European companies travelling in South America that optimized transportation and personnel costs. This plan allowed companies, their singing stars, and of course the STIA to operate at peak efficiency and thereby increase profits. As Mocchi's own magazine *Il Teatro illustrato* remarked:

> The companies will no longer cross the Ocean … to find themselves in trouble after playing in Buenos Aires or on their short journeys to Rosario or Montevideo: they will have the guarantee of a long and logically organized tour.[58]

Organizing the South American circulation of artists was not easy: the distances between the STIA's venues were considerable. For example, in 1909 the Grande Compagnia Lirica Italiana, conducted by Luigi Mancinelli and Giuseppe Baroni, performed at the Colón, then travelled to Santiago de Chile and Valparaiso. The company then returned to Buenos Aires to perform at the Coliseo, the Avenida, and other secondary venues.

The STIA offered a wide range of repertory. Mocchi catered to various immigrant communities with specific troupes, such as the company of Carlo Nunziata, which performed in the Neapolitan dialect, and the Spanish zarzuela company led by Emilio Sagi-Barba (1876–1949), the baritone-impresario who created the role of Danilo in Lehár's *La viuda alegre* (*The Merry Widow*) in Madrid in 1909. Mocchi's cooperation with Sagi-Barba did not last, since the Italian impresario preferred to invest in operetta rather than zarzuela.

Operetta began to play an increasing role in Mocchi's activities. He brought major Italian operetta companies such as Scognamiglio, Caramba, and Marchetti, as well as the German company, Pakque, to South America and engaged the leading Italian composer of the genre, Luigi Dall'Argine (1873–1950), as conductor. Most of these companies belonged or were tightly

---

[57] Although Ciacchi signed the agreement, the STIA took over as an administrative partner. For his part, the impresario received a cheque for 110,000 pesos, a monthly salary of 1,000 pesos, and 20 per cent of the profits. R. Caamaño, *La historia del Teatro Colón 1908–1968* (Cinetea, 1969), vol. III, p. 75.

[58] *Il Teatro Illustrato*, 15 November 1907 "La grande Società teatrale Italo Argentina".

connected to the publishers Suvini Zerboni and Sonzogno, which mandated their own repertoire and their own Italian translations. South American audiences enjoyed the greatest successes from the Viennese and French operetta stages (Lehár, Straus, Suppé, Offenbach, Varney, Lecocq), as well as féeries, parodies, and a handful of British works (Leslie Stuart, Sidney Jones, but no Gilbert and Sullivan, whose copyright in Italy was held by the competitor Ricordi). According to critics, these companies performed 'with indescribable success in theatres that were completely sold out, and the sale of season ticket exceeded all expectations'.[59] Even Mocchi's rival impresario Giuseppe Paradossi had to confess that Mocchi's operetta scheme earned 'a triumphal welcome and strong earnings. For operetta it is the golden age'.[60]

One major challenge for the STIA tours was that stage sets could only travel by river or by train. Potential delays constantly put the next production at risk. A late delivery of the sets could force the management either to keep the venue closed or to mount reruns. The latter happened in August 1909 at the Colón, when the announced premiere of *Les Huguenots* by the Grande Compagnia Lirica Italiana, conducted by Luigi Mancinelli, had to be replaced at the very last moment by *The Damnation of Faust*, which had already had a long run. The audience strongly protested, causing the conductor Mancinelli to stop the performance. Ciacchi entered the stage to calm the protesters, but the end result was shattering:

> The show was suspended and the audience went to the box office for refunds
> .... The Trust has no more sympathy nor defenders: Mancinelli and the
> artists condemned the Colón management .... It is going to be the death of a
> badly run Association that has never done anything for the Art nor for its
> income.[61]

The STIA maintained its leading role in the South American market for just a couple of years, from 1907 to 1909. While this might not seem like a long time, the effects of the organization were immense. Its extensive network brought together theatre managers and touring companies into a single enterprise, the ultimate aim of which was to minimize costs and maximize profits. But the question remains, did it work in terms of having a long-term financial sustainability?

The answer is probably not. No complete company archive survives, and some accounting documents are extant in the STIN archive in Rome. These documents provide a partial view of the South American enterprise and do not

---

[59] 'Notizie e varietà', *Il Teatro Illustrato*, 1–31 August 1910. The article refers to the success of
Giulio Marchetti's company.

[60] G. Paradossi, 'La grave crisi delle compagnie drammatiche nell'America del Sud', *Il Teatro
Illustrato*, 1–15 October 1909.

[61] 'Scandale à l'Opéra', *Comœdia*, 22 August 1909.

include data on single performances. However, the Argentine press seemed curious about the STIA's mysterious financial results. Unable to obtain any private accounting documents, the magazine *Comœdia* cleverly investigated the royalties paid to the copyright collecting agency, which was public information. Although tax avoidance should be taken into account, the analysis offered some illuminating remarks:

> I have spoken about the Colon, which in fourteen months has lost less than 26,500,000 francs some people say 60,000,000, and it might be .... The Odéon is the most profitable of the theatres of the trust. For every performance of the major companies it pays 250 francs in royalties. The Avenida has the worst deal in this extraordinary company: just 2% is paid to the Copyright collecting agency .... The Coliseo imposes silence on itself for its overruns. Le Variedades ... closed its doors eight days after its opening.[62]

It seems that each theatre, at least in Buenos Aires, had different results. Some, like the Odeón, did well, while most did not. Looking at STIN's ledgers, this analysis is confirmed. STIA controlled the market in terms of agreements, venues, and repertoire but did not succeed in fully accomplishing its financial goal of making a profitable business of theatre.

Part of this failure could be due to the fact that certain productions were expected to lose money, but since these works formed part of a package, the hope was that more popular titles in the package would offset losses. (This strategy is still practised today — theatre and opera companies will offer a hugely popular work that they hope will sell out so that they can use the profits from that production to help cover losses from a less-familiar work that might sell fewer tickets.) As an example, when Lugné-Poe's Théâtre de l'Œuvre tour failed miserably at Buenos Aires's Avenida Theatre in 1909, the troupe's namesake lead actor and director described himself as a victim of the STIA's 'trust of theatre owners'.[63]

In 1909 the STIA was already showing signs of decline. That year, Séguin resigned as CEO of the 'Sociedad',[64] even though he remained active in some of the underhanded financing of its activities. It suffered a decisive blow on 5 June 1911, when the Argentine Government withdrew the STIA's licence to operate as a limited company.[65] The enterprise, however, continued to function as a corporate entity: its underhanded power played a decisive role in the awarding of the municipal grant for the Colón in 1912, which Cesare Ciacchi (who had

---

[62] V. Demarzat, 'Le trust des Théâtres à Buenos-Ayres', *Comœdia*, 1 September 1909.

[63] Lugné Poe, *La Parade:Sous les etoiles. Souvenirs de théâtre (1902–1912)* (Gallimard, 1933), p. 248.

[64] *Boletin Oficial de la República Argentina*, a. XVII, n. 4735, 13 September 1909.

[65] *Boletin Oficial de la República Argentina,* a. XIX, n. 5238, 7 June 1911.

held it previously) received at the end of a complicated wrangle between the 'Sociedad' and its competitors. Meanwhile Séguin started a new enterprise of his own, the South American Tour, that featured 'spettacoli di arte varia',[66] tangos, and wrestling matches. Mocchi, though, continued to build his theatrical empire. Although the STIA would remain active until 1912, in 1910 he took out his own corporate capital in order to establish a new company, La Teatral, which ensured him personal control over several venues on both sides of the Atlantic. In order to secure the success of La Teatral, however, he first needed to create and control a similar enterprise to the STIA, but one based in Italy.

3. Mocchi in Italy: The Early Years of the Società Teatrale Internazionale

To maximize the potential for the interoceanic theatrical trade between Europe and South America, the Sociedad Teatral Ítalo-Argentina (STIA) needed an Italian branch. This was established in Rome on 24 July 1908, under the name Società Teatrale Internazionale (STIN, see Figure 3.1).[67] Despite the strong influence of the STIA, the STIN was an independent entity with a slightly different purpose. Compared to the STIA, the Italian venture had a broader base of shareholders and in its early days not only managed theatres and tours but also sponsored the creation of new works.

The establishment of the STIN was hailed as a cultural rebirth for the troubled Italian theatre industry. As noted in the press: 'With this company, which can be genuinely trusted because of the importance of its promoting personalities, the Italian art . . . may once again count on its full forces'.[68] The company was established in a hall at the Conservatory Accademia di Santa Cecilia by a mixed group of speculators, entrepreneurs, music publishers, composers, and wealthy opera lovers. The aim of the joint-stock company was to 'develop the theatrical industry in the broadest way, without any exclusions

---

[66] This was a special kind of show performed in Category II and III theatres that included cabaret, musical numbers, dance, and comedy sketches.

[67] The STIN lasted until 1931, making it one of the longest-lasting entities in the history of Italian theatre. Although the STIN began in the private sector it ended up as a state-controlled enterprise. Its existence can be divided into four periods: (1) from 1908 to 1911, the company created a trust among the main theatres in Italy, Pietro Mascagni was engaged as general manager of the Costanzi in Rome, and the financial losses of some theatrical seasons caused the board to focus on their properties in Rome and Turin; (2) in 1911 the STIN became a corporate tool with which to control the Costanzi, the company's main asset; (3) in 1912 La Teatral, a company founded by Mocchi and Carelli (discussed in Section 4) acquired the majority shares, thus making them the owners of the Costanzi; and (4) in 1926 the fascist Government of Rome became the majority shareholder and transformed the Costanzi into the sumptuous Teatro Reale dell'Opera, inaugurated in 1928. This section focuses on only the first phase of the STIN.

[68] 'La nuova società teatrale', *Il Secolo*, 15 June 1908.

Figure 3.1 First meeting of the STIN's board of directors at the STIA's agency in Milan. (*Il Teatro illustrato*)

whatsoever'.[69] STIN decided to establish its base in Milan, where the northern location could allow the company to negotiate better agreements and cut brokerage costs.

Mocchi's magazine, *Il Teatro illustrato* (The Illustrated Theatre), was quick to hail the importance of the trust and its owners:

> The colossal revolution of theatrical market, its quick evolution into the kingdom of great industry [and] the introduction of the capitalistic regime that replaced the primitive stage marked by isolated impresarios without any money or artistic criteria who worked in the theatre as though at a gambling exploitation, a baccarat, a roulette; the establishment of a system that is rooted in the millions [of lire] that are invested in theatre as though as they were in the iron or oil trade, as well as the purpose of erasing competition, reducing operating costs, abolishing middlemen and parasites . . . Hence, this colossal revolution of theatrical commerce was the ingenious idea for which Walter Mocchi did not only have the creative spark but also the prodigious [ability to make it happen]. All of it is accomplished, and no human resistance will ever counteract or impede it.[70]

---

[69] 'Costituzione della Società Teatrale Internazionale', *Bollettino ufficiale per le Società per Azioni*, n. XXVII, 27 August 1908.

[70] 'S.T.I.A.-S.T.I.N.', *Il Teatro Illustrato*, 5 November 1908.

Beyond the high rhetoric, the article pointed out the novelty of Mocchi's visionary project and its possible impact on the Italian market. This was at a time when the public thought of a 'trust' as a new obsession associated with the young century. As one journalist noted, 'it's a mania!'[71] Influenced by the US model, in Italy the word 'trust' generally meant 'any attempted abuse of a dominant position'.[72] The topic became so popular that Luigi Dall'Argine composed an operetta on it (*Amor trust* (Love Trust), 1909).

Although there had already been some attempts at creating a theatrical trust in Italy (in 1904 Enrico di San Martino had tried to form a 'Società Anonima Italiana per il teatro lirico'[73]), the establishment of the STIN, though exciting, had its dangers. The certificate of incorporation set no limits: the company could build or purchase theatres ('as well as venues for opera, drama, or any other genre, in Italy or abroad'), create shops for scenery, costumes and props, and engage 'artists, maestros, ... companies, choruses, orchestras and choirs'.[74] Even though the word 'trust' never appears in the official documents, the society's objective was certainly clear, as Enrico di San Martino, the STIN's president, noted:

> Here is our project: nowadays every theatre is forced to bear on its own expensive contracts with the artists and huge expenses for the staging, for which by now the audience has developed extraordinary demands . . . . When our federation will have gathered together all the main theatres in Italy, we will just need one magnificent and singular staging that will be used in all the cities where we will take our shows. The artists will have to accept more specific conditions, considering that they will be engaged for the whole year or maybe longer.[75]

The basic systemic plan, as San Martino articulated it, bore a very close similarity to that of the STIA in South America.

The STIN was established with a very large share capital (L. 2,000,000 divided in 400 shares of L. 5,000 each; about €8 million in 2019) that reflected the ambition of its founders. Two large groups emerged within the STIN, each of which promoted a somewhat different vision and strategy for the company. On one side was the Sociedad Teatral Ítalo-Argentina, owner of two fifths of the shares (160) and which was simply interested in making a profit. On the other side was a mixed group of Italians who held the relative majority and swayed between speculation and aristocratic patronage. Members of this influential

---

[71] 'Trust su tutta la linea', *L'Arte Melodrammatica*, 30 September 1907.

[72] L. Cavaglieri, *Trust teatrali e diritto d'autore (1894–1910). La tentazione del monopolio* (Titivillus, 2012), p. 35.

[73] 'Il "trust" del teatro lirico in Italia', *La Stampa*, 29 January 1904. The project was also announced as 'Società per il teatro lirico italiano', or 'Federazione dei teatri italiani'.

[74] 'Costituzione della Società Teatrale Internazionale'.

[75] 'Una conversazione col conte di San Martino', *Il Teatro Illustrato*, 21 June–5 July 1908.

second group included the director of the Accademia di Santa Cecilia, Enrico di San Martino (23 shares); the impresario of the Teatro San Carlo of Naples, Roberto de Sanna (53); the publisher Edoardo Sonzogno (42) and his associate Friedrich Erlanger (4); the industrialists and politicians Ettore Bocconi (12), Riccardo Biglia (10), Tullo Cantoni (11), Luigi Cantoni (6), and Guido Ravà Sforni (22); the conductor Louis Lombard (42); the composer Giacomo Orefice (4); and the president of the Teatro alla Scala, Uberto Visconti di Modrone (11). These individuals were first and foremost interested in building and sustaining a holistic theatrical ecosystem in Italy.

The STIN operated as a multi-divisional body, with a board of directors controlling several semi-autonomous units (individual theatres).[76] The board appointed Mocchi as general agent, meaning that he oversaw the relationship between management and operations, managing the partnership between the STIA and STIN with the aid of Renzo Sonzogno.

To gain control of the Italian theatres, the company replicated the strategy successfully used in South America with STIA: agreements were made with the impresarios who ran the municipal halls, each of whom underhandedly trans-ferred their municipal grants to STIN, after which the board appointed them directors of their respective theatres. Although this practice was illegal, the municipal authorities accepted it because of the prestige of STIN's shareholders and the financial integrity of the trust, which seemed to them more reliable and secure than one single and impecunious impresario.[77]

Thanks to this strategy, within a few months the STIN had acquired the main opera houses in Italy: the Teatro Regio in Turin, the Teatro Regio in Parma, the Carlo Felice in Genoa, the Argentina and the Adriano in Rome, and the Petruzzelli in Bari.[78] The STIN seemed to choose these venues both for their prestige and for their municipal grants; except for the Petruzzelli and the Adriano (which were run by the same impresario, Antonio Quaranta, and abandoned after a single season) all the theatres controlled by the STIN received public funding, which accounted for 7 to 42 per cent of the revenues for their operatic seasons (see Table 3.1).

---

[76] ASC, *STIN*, b. 3, f. 7, *Regolamento Interno della Società Teatrale Internazionale Anonima con Capitale di Lire 2.000.000.*

[77] The impresarios earned a yearly salary of between L. 6,000 and 18,000 (depending on the importance of the venue) and received 3 per cent of the gross income and 10 to 30 per cent of the net revenues for the season.

[78] For the 1908–1909 season, the theatres were run by a director (first name listed) and an administrator (second name listed) as follows. Teatro Costanzi: Giacomo Orefice and Gino Rossetti; Regio di Torino: Temistocle Pozzali and Carlo Körner; Carlo Felice: Ercole Casali and Arturo Bruno; Regio di Parma: Delfino Legnani and Gennaro D'Angelo; Petruzzelli: Antonio Quaranta and Alberto Pereira.

Table 3.1 Revenues and costs for the 1908–1909 season in the STIN's opera houses. The financial statement of the Petruzzelli (Bari) is missing from the archive. Author's elaboration on STIN's financial statements (ASC, *STIN*, b. 5, f. 1)

STIN Opera season	Teatro Costanzi (Rome)		Teatro Regio (Turin)		Teatro Carlo Felice (Genoa)		Teatro Regio (Parma)	
Revenues	**653,689**		**288,406**		**219,034**		**119,007**	
Tickets	234,397	35.86%	147,531	51.15%	94,312	43.06%	52.576	44.18%
Season tickets	258,016	39.47%	92,262	31.99%	10,995	5.02%	39.450	33.15%
Public funds	80,000	12.23%	20,000	6.93%	92,962	42.44%	22.000	18.49%
Operating costs	**693,892**		**289,670**		**243,414**		**178,591**	
Orchestra	78,427	11.30%	Granted by the municipality		50,462	20.73%	31.655	17.72%
Singers	288,840	41.63%	114,753	39.62%	66,649	27.38%	55.749	31.22%
Conductors	29,365	4.23%	4,021	1.39%	4.286	1.76%	10.477	5.87%
Choir	41,842	6.03%	23,124	7.98%	20.926	8.60%	18.404	10.31%
Dancers & choreographer	14,894	2.15%	7,571	2.61%	6,505	2.67%	4,398	2.46%
Scenery and costumes	19,996	2.88%	23,800	8.22%	19,487	8.01%	9,927	5.56%
Copyright	49,910	7.19%	22,015	7.60%	16,850	6.92%	14,572	8.16%

Contracting with impresarios was not the only way STIN acquired theatres. Less than a week after its founding, the trust purchased Rome's main opera house, the Teatro Costanzi, for L. 2,300,000. This was considered a reckless operation that had been made possible through a L 1,200,000 loan from the Società Bancaria Italiana. The Costanzi would play a pivotal role in the history of the STIN and indeed in the entire realm of Italian theatrical economics.

Rome thus became STIN's main market. Besides owning the Costanzi, the STIN directly controlled the popular Politeama Adriano and the city's main dramatic theatre (the Argentina), and it indirectly influenced the largest concert hall in the city, the Corea Theatre (managed by the Accademia di Santa Cecilia and under the firm control of by Enrico di San Martino until his death in 1947). San Martino, who became a Senatore del Regno d'Italia (senator of the kingdom) in 1911, oversaw the STIN's Roman activities while also serving as the municipal commissioner for fine arts, vice-president of the Roman Society of Authors, and president of the Drammatica Compagnia di Roma (also known as Stabile Romana, an entity founded in 1905 and to which the municipality granted the free use of the Teatro Argentina).

The Teatro Argentina played an unusual role in the STIN, since it was at the time a dramatic theatre and not a musical one. The historic venue boasted a glorious past, including the premiere of Rossini's *Il barbiere di Siviglia* in 1816. The STIN wanted the house as part of its network; so, shortly after its establishment, it purchased 15,000 shares of the Drammatica Compagnia for the modest amount of L. 80,000 in order to gain control of the venue.[79] In this opulent theatre, the primary pursuit was visual splendour, as explained by San Martino:

> The carpets will be all new and specially woven in Brussels: pure wool . . . .
> All the furniture brand new . . .. The columns will be columns, the windows
> will be made of glass: I hope that Garavaglia [the leading actor] will break a
> couple of them, to show the audience that I have suppressed all the fake
> stagery . . . . I also bought some new pendant and table lamps that the audience
> has never seen: for *Giulio Cesare* just electric lamps . . . .[80]

San Martino was keen to bring a sense of stage realism and naturalism to the theatre's productions, following the inspiration of George II of Saxe-Meiningen and André Antoine. His idea never materialized.

---

[79] The Teatro Argentina opened on 3 January 1732, and immediately became the most important stage in Rome, for both spoken drama and opera. In 1869 it became the property of the municipality. After the opening of the Teatro Costanzi in 1880, the Argentina suffered from competition with the new venue, mostly in terms of opera. S. Severi, *I teatri di Roma* (Newton Compton, 1989), pp. 70–9.

[80] 'Alla vigilia dell'apertura dell'Argentina: Un'intervista col Conte di San Martino', *L'Arte Drammatica*, 2 December 1905.

On 8 August 1908 STIN appointed Enrico Polese-Santarnecchi general manager of the Drammatica Compagnia di Roma. Polese was a theatrical agent and editor of the major theatrical magazine in Italy, *L'Arte Drammatica*, as well as the director of the spoken-drama department of the STIA. The situation he found at the Teatro Argentina was not a straightforward one: 'the company was completely demoralized by the violent attacks from the press ... and you can't imagine the anarchy that was ruling in the theatre. I had to be a watchdog!'[81] The Argentina's life as part of the STIN started on 10 August 1908, just two days after Polese's appointment, with a performance of Gabriele d'Annunzio's *La Nave* (The Ship). The timing was terrible, for the city emptied during the summer holidays, and in August most companies moved to the holiday resorts in order to perform for the vacationing urban audiences. This was not an option for the Argentina. Polese recalled:

> the company had no repertoire of its own and couldn't go on tour, not even for just twenty performances .... So, I chose to stage *La Nave*, for which we held the performing rights, by considerably reducing the expenses for supernumeraries, dancers, and singers. I also offered popular [e.g. lower] prices .... The audience responded well.[82]

To reduce expenses and make quick profits, Polese planned a popular season so that the company – under the direction of its leading actor Cesare Dondini – could start to perform basically without rehearsals. The newest dramas were excluded, not only because they would have required rehearsals, but also because 'the moment [was] not favourable for dramatic theatre: the Italian as well as the French theatre ha[d] few great writers, and for ages we ha[d] been longing for the longed masterpiece'.[83] Once the season was underway, Polese contacted the main importer of French plays, Adolfo Re Riccardi, to secure new works for the Argentina. His most controversial choice was Pierre-Samuel Berton's and Charles Simon's *Zazà*, a ten-year-old play about a prostitute who becomes a music hall entertainer and the mistress of a married man. *Zazà* certainly attracted an audience, but was judged improper for performance by a publicly funded dramatic company. Polese and Mocchi, in their quest for publicity, seemed to have planned the controversy. The previous year, Mocchi's wife, soprano Emma Carelli, had sung Ruggero Leoncavallo's operatic version of *Zazà* at the Teatro Verdi in Trieste. The police had to stop the performance after a fight erupted between the opera chorus and the audience when the spectators challenged Carelli for 'imposing the opera' on them and 'being the

---

[81] ASC, *STIN*, b. 1, f. 9, Report by Enrico Polese to the board of directors, 24 October 1908.
[82] Ibid.   [83] Ibid.

wife of a socialist leader'.[84] Now, at the Argentina, the Italian Author Society passed a motion against Polese,[85] while the municipality protested against the 'new management of the Teatro Argentina, which had become a useless duplicate of the Manzoni and the Metastasio', referring to two famed commercial venues in Rome.[86] Of course this type of press coverage would only bring more people to the Argentina.

Musical theatre, however, not spoken drama, was the core business of the STIN, and the opera season provided its most prestigious offerings. The main opera season in Italy, Carnival season, began in December and lasted until the late spring of the following year. For the STIN's first season, 1908–09, it hired composer Giacomo Orefice to plan its offerings. Much of the season had already been set under previous managers, and in the summer of 1908 the STIN had to honour several pre-existing agreements, contracts with singers, and choices of work in order to start the season on time. Many of the opera productions, including the singers, had been touring South America through the STIA and continued to perform in Italy under the STIN.

To emphasize the importance of its first opera season, the trust invested heavily in its major venues. At the Costanzi, Giorgio Polacco, who in seven years would succeed Arturo Toscanini as conductor of the Metropolitan Opera in New York, was appointed principal conductor. As an additional mark of prestige Michael Balling came from Bayreuth to conduct the grand opening night on 26 December 1908 with *La Valchiria* (*Die Walküre*).[87] Wagner's operas, in Italian translation, also opened STIN seasons in Genoa and Turin.

To put its forward-looking vision into practice, the STIN gave its audiences the opportunity to see new works during the inaugural opera season. These included the Roman premiere of Debussy's *Pelléas et Mélisande* (Teatro Costanzi, 29 March 1909) and the world premieres of Franco Alfano's *Il Principe Zilah* (Prince Zilah, Teatro Carlo Felice, Genoa, 3 February 1909), and Italo Montemezzi's *Héllera* (Teatro Regio, Turin, 17 March 1909). The plan backfired; all three works were poorly received. Debussy's *Pelléas et Mélisande* was described as 'a vile holocaust', and the critic noted that 'the symbolist and obscure music was annihilated by . . . laughter, screams, jokes, hisses'.[88]

[84] 'Una serata tumultuosa al teatro Verdi di Trieste', *La Stampa*, 3 February 1907.

[85] 'La questione dell'Argentina alla Società degli Autori', *Giornale d'Italia*, 23 October 1908.

[86] 'Il programma "artistico" dell'Argentina: Un energico richiamo del Municipio', *Giornale d'Italia*, 15 October 1908.

[87] Balling was engaged from 7 December 1908 to 31 January 1909 at a salary of L. 5,000. (ASC, *STIN*, b. 2, f. 8, Agreement between Giacomo Orefice and Michael Balling, 19 August 1908).

[88] N. d'Atri, '"Pelleas e Melisanda" di C. Debussy: Tempestosa serata al Costanzi', *Giornale d'Italia*, 30 March 1909.

Singers included some of the biggest stars from Italy along with less-familiar names who had made their careers in South America. Among the singing stars were such notable names as Salomea Krusceniski, Carlo Walter, Eugenia Burzio, Giannina Russ, Titta Ruffo, Manfredi Polverosi, and of course Emma Carelli. Carelli, after singing two performances in Mascagni's *Iris* at the Regio in Turin, declared herself indisposed after a disagreement with the local theatre impresario, Temiscole Pozzali. The STIN's official administrator in Turin, Carlo Körner, criticized Carelli's behaviour, and since she was representing Mocchi's interests in the city, Körner was fired. Carelli's place in Mocchi's empire was higher than Körner's. The South American singers certainly helped lower the cost of the payroll with their appearances, though some critics became dismayed at the lack of recognizable names:

> I will not complain if the usual *cantante cannone* (singing star) was missing, because it merely represented the artistic quackery that arouses enthusiasm in the 'parvenus' that compose the South American audience, that throws away hundred thousands of Lire for a tenor as it does for a racing horse, while it understands neither the first nor the latter. I will complain because when the operas are staged, nobody cares – and that is common – about the different nature of each singer.[89]

A perhaps unexpected effect resulted from the presence of lesser-known artists. Audiences demanded star performers, which led to an 'excessive raise of the payrolls' for the famed Italian singers, a move that was criticized by the press.[90]

The STIN's inaugural opera season, from a financial standpoint, was a failure. (See Table 3.1.) The failures of the new works and the Italian singers' salary demands certainly contributed to the overall deficit. Neither the prestige of the costly principals nor the popularity of the repertoire (e.g. *Aida*, *Madama Butterfly*, *Rigoletto*) could increase the revenue. On 30 June 1909, the first financial statement recorded a general deficit of L. 464,685.02, of which L. 293,845.98 was attributed to specific theatres.[91] The newly formed trust was not alone in its losses, for the Teatro alla Scala also ended up with a 'financial disaster' at the end of its 1908–1909 season.[92]

Several additional factors contributed to the STIN's deficit, including the fact that parts of the season were already in place when the trust was established and

[89] '"Rigoletto" al Costanzi', *Avanti!*, 13 January 1909.

[90] N. d'Atri, 'La "Gioconda" al Costanzi. Discutendo un po' di divi', *Giornale d'Italia*, 2 April 1909.

[91] The worst-performing theatre was the Petruzzelli (-82,210.41), followed by the Regio di Parma (-61,359.75), the Politeama Adriano (-60,393.40), the Regio di Torino (-51,905.90), and the Carlo Felice (-27,236.35).

[92] I. Piazzoni, *Dal 'Teatro dei palchettisti' all'Ente autonomo: la Scala, 1897–1920* (La Nuova Italia, 1995), p. 149.

that it had had to honour agreements already made with other managers. The STIN realized the difficulty of cobbling together a season from many moving and some stationary parts, confessing that its challenges included 'an insufficient and unprepared organization, which no one can be blamed for, because of the novelty and complexity of our management'.[93] The most serious problems concerned the scheduling of productions and getting them from one city to the next. In Turin, for instance, the debuts of Emma Carelli in Mascagni's *Iris* and Giannina Russ in Bellini's *Norma* seemed to set the season on the right track, but due to a pre-existent agreement, Bellini's opera, which was playing at the Regio, had to be taken to Parma after only three nights. The cast and sets for the incoming opera at the Regio, Montemezzi's *Héllera*, were stuck in Genoa and could not get to Turin, which meant that the Regio had to stay closed. Incidents such as this all contributed to the season's financial losses.

Nature played its part as well. On 28 December 1908, at the very beginning of the season, a devastating earthquake in Messina forced the theatres to remain closed for an extended period of mourning. No performances, no income. Then in February, an extraordinary snowfall shut down the railways, making it impossible to transport casts and scenery from one place to another.

Among the STIN's theatres, only the Costanzi was able to minimize its liabilities (to L. 10,740.17), something it accomplished by offsetting its costs with residencies by two operetta companies, the Città di Genova and the Città di Milano. 'The operetta season ... considerably decreased our losses', admitted Alberto Marghieri, the STIN's chief executive officer.[94] Both companies were owned by Suvini Zerboni and had substantial financial footings. The Città di Genova had an orchestra of thirty-six players, a singing chorus of fifty-five, a dance troupe of eighteen, and a repertoire that extended from Viennese operettas given in Italian (*La vedova allegra* (*The Merry Widow*), *Un sogno di valzer* [*A Waltz Dream*]) to works by Rossini and Donizetti, along with féeries (e.g. Carlo Lombardo's *La polvere di Pirlimpinpin* [*The Powder of Pirlimpinpin*]) and musical parodies of contemporary politics (e.g. Renato Simoni's *Turlupineide*, the most successful title of the entire season). The Città di Genova's conductor was Carlo Lombardo (1869–1959), who conducted his own féerie during the season, mentioned above, and later would enter operetta annals as the creator of the important Italian operetta *Il paese dei campanelli* (*The Village of Bells*, 1923). The Città di Milano was called 'a marvellous ensemble: sceneries, costumes, voices, everything was out of the ordinary in operetta terms'.[95] Its star was Emma Vecla (1877–1972), the Algerian-born

[93] ASC, *STIN*, b. 5, fasc. 1, *Relazione fatta dall'Amministratore Generale della Stin al Consiglio d'Amministrazione. Seduta del 5 aprile 1909.*
[94] Ibid.　[95] 'Al Costanzi', *Il Tirso*, 6 September 1908.

French soprano responsible for the astonishing success of *The Merry Widow*'s Italian premiere. Vecla began performing in STIN theatres immediately after Franz Lehár congratulated her in Milan for her success. Città di Genova showcased scenery by the La Scala painter Antonio Rovescalli, and both companies featured the lavish costumes of Luigi Sapelli, also known as Caramba, the famed costumer for Teatro alla Scala. Both companies offered visual feasts, whether it was the glitz and gaiety of operetta or the impassioned romance of more traditional Italian operas. As one critic noted:

> Last night the Città di Milano left behind the phantasmagorical scenery, the choreographic grandiosity, the glitz multiplied by the singing masses and by the chorus line; it left behind all that whole of glittering richness that too often dresses the musical poverty of modern operettas, that seem almost trans-formed into cinema, with living colours and poor ideas. Last night we moved back to a masterpiece . . ., *Don Pasquale* . . . favourably staged at the Costanzi . . . with artistic beauty.[96]

Critics were surprised at the success of the operetta season, noting not just the large numbers of attendees but also the atypical audience behaviour at the Costanzi:

> Last night the renowned *Geisha* was staged, an operetta that with its grace collects from the non-discerning audience unfading success, thus bringing to the cash register of the impresarios a great amount of money. The turnout of the audience was enormous, partly because of a decrease in the ticket prices. But the crowd in the *loggione* (gallery) was particularly excited; after having enjoyed some encores during the first two acts, they demanded more during the 'couplets' of Mr Favi, who fulfilled their thirst to the limits of his patience . . . . He did not consider that a certain kind of audience – especially one for the *Geisha* – is not used to theatrical conventions.[97]

This was not a unique critical response:

> I believe it never happened before that a performance had to be interrupted due to the excessive enthusiasm of the audience. But we had to see this too . . . . To calm the overly extreme admiration of the audience sitting in the *piccionaia* (gallery), it would be enough, I suppose, to double the ticket prices and the guards[.][98]

The popular genre of operetta, pure and simple, was critical in minimizing the losses of the STIN's first season. A new audience was coming to the Costanzi. Money was to be made here, and the revenues from the Costanzi proved it. For

---

[96] '"Don Pasquale" al Costanzi', *Avanti!*, 14 November 1908.
[97] 'Una gazzarra al Costanzi per la "Geisha"', *Avanti!*, 16 October 1908.
[98] G. De Frenzi, 'La Ghescia al Teatro Costanzi', *Giornale d'Italia*, 16 October 1908.

the operetta season, box-office receipts counted for 96 per cent and season tickets for 2.51 per cent, whereas for the opera season, these figures were 35 per cent and 39 per cent (see Table 3.2.) The performances by the Città di Milano alone produced 43.01 per cent of the opera season's total revenues, without any public funding.

Mocchi realized the potential of operetta as a money-making genre and the crucial role it could play in the STIN enterprise. In 1910, the STIN refused municipal funding for the Costanzi, giving up its opera season, and rented the theatre to the Scognamiglio–Caramba Company with an agreement that gave 65 per cent of the revenues to the operetta company and 35 per cent to the STIN, which provided the thirty-six-member orchestra. As Renzo Sonzogno himself suggested: 'I would consider it appropriate that our Company would not let the Scognamiglio–Caramba Company slip away, because it is the only one that may decently substitute for the Carnival opera season'.[99] The success of operetta reinforced the exchange of companies between STIN and STIA to the extent that a special clause was added to the agreement between the two trusts:

> The Società Teatrale Italo Argentina grants the Società Teatrale Internazionale exclusive rights for the South American market for the branches of straight theatre and operetta, meaning that no dramatic or operetta company from Italy will be allowed to perform in the theatres held by the Società Teatrale Italo Argentina if they are not under control of the Società Teatrale Internazionale.[100]

Despite the success of its operettas, the STIN struggled. In spring 1909, most of its Italian shareholders were concerned about losing money, and some of them asked San Martino to fold the company to avoid the personal disgrace of a possible bankruptcy. That summer, several foreign investors showed interest in forming a French branch of the company 'pour l'exploitation d'une Salle de Spectacle située au centre même de Paris' (for the exploitation of a showplace located in the very centre of Paris).[101] This did not happen because in the meantime the STIA, the other shareholding group in the STIN, acquired the Teatro Colón in Buenos Aires and became 'the exclusive referee of the South American artistic market' and achieved 'the monopoly it [had] aimed to create'.[102]

The STIN's management underscored the importance of 'harmonizing and coordinating the theatrical exchange between Italy and South America'[103]

---

[99] ASC, *STIN*, b. 4, f. 4, Letter from Renzo Sonzogno to Alberto Marghieri, 21 February 1910.

[100] ASC, *STIN*, b. 5, f. 1, *Assemblea generale 16–28 gennaio 1908*.

[101] ASC, *STIN*, b. 3, f. 29, *Notice sur un projet de 'Théâtre International'*.

[102] 'L'"Opera" di Buenos Ayres chiude i battenti', *Giornale d'Italia*, 7 April 1909.

[103] ASC, *STIN*, b. 5, f. 1, *Relazione fatta dall'Amministratore Generale della Stin al Consiglio d'Amministrazione*.

Table 3.2 Revenues and costs of 1908–1909 season at the Costanzi. Author's elaboration on STIN's financial statements (ASC, *STIN*, b. 5, f. 1).

	Opera Season		Operetta season "Città di Milano"	
Revenues	6,53,689		2,81,147	
Box office (individual tickets)	2,34,395	35.86%	2,72,216	96.82%
Season tickets	2,58,016	39.47%	7,063	2.51%
Season box seat rental	56,341	8.62%	0	0.00%
Public funding	79,995	12.24%	0	0.00%
Other income	24,907	3.81%	1,868	0.66%
Operating costs	6,93,892		2,67,763	
Performances	74		66	
Cost per performance	9,377		4,057	
Orchestra	78,427	11.30%	15,394	5.75%
Singers	2,88,840	41.63%		
Conductors	29,365	4.23%		
Choir	41,842	6.03%		
Dancers & choreographer	14,894	2.15%	1,90,263	71.06%
Scenery	19,996	2.88%		
Copyright	49,910	7.19%		
Services (lighting, box office, cleaning, etc.)	1,70,618	24.59%	62,106	23.19%

Opera Season – Productions in profit

Teatro Costanzi Season 1908–09	Aida		Madama Butterfly		La Damnation De Faust		Hamlet		Gioconda	
Revenues	1,23,265		67,843		68,922		45,626		59,448	
Individual tickets	60,502	49.08%	18,157	26.76%	19,236	27.91%	17,557	38.48%	22,750	38.27%
Season tickets	32,252	26.16%	32,252	47.54%	32,252	46.79%	19,351	42.41%	25,802	43.40%
Season box seat rental	10,660	8.65%	6,091	8.98%	6,091	8.84%	3,045	6.67%	3,807	6.40%
Public funding	15,135	12.28%	8,648	12.75%	8,648	12.55%	4,324	9.48%	5,405	9.09%
Other income	4,713	3.82%	2,693	3.97%	2,693	3.91%	1,346	2.95%	1,683	2.83%
Operating costs	1,08,625		65,681		65,125		37,202		57,377	
Performances	14		8		8		4		5	
Cost per performance	7,759		8,210		8,141		9,301		11,475	
Orchestra	12,800	11.78%	7,314	11.14%	7,314	11.23%	3,657	9.83%	4,571	7.97%
Singers	40,156	36.97%	29,296	44.60%	20,633	31.68%	15,055	40.47%	24,932	43.45%
Conductors	4,795	4.41%	2,740	4.17%	2,740	4.21%	1,370	3.68%	1,712	2.98%
Choir	7,916	7.29%	4,523	6.89%	4,523	6.95%	2,261	6.08%	2,827	4.93%
Dancers & choreographer	5,086	4.68%	0	0.00%	2,906	4.46%	1,453	3.91%	1,816	3.17%
Scenery	1,049	0.97%	539	0.82%	2,190	3.36%	243	0.65%	3,185	5.55%
Copyright	5,260	4.84%	6,250	9.52%	5,000	7.68%	2,000	5.38%	5,000	8.71%
Services	31,563	29.06%	15,019	22.87%	19,819	30.43%	11,163	30.01%	13,334	23.24%

Table 3.2 (cont.)

Opera Season – Productions in loss

	Die Walküre		Rigoletto		Andrea Chénier		Pelleas et Melisande		Il Principe Zilah		Rhea		Loreley	
Revenues	92,296		47,996		67,492		13,143		23,825		29,069		14,753	
Individual tickets	38,251	41.44%	24,112	50.24%	17,806	26.38%	4,513	34.34%	4,387	18.41%	3,180	10.94%	3,944	26.73%
Season tickets	32,253	34.95%	6,450	13.44%	32,252	47.79%	6,450	49.08%	12,901	54.15%	19,351	66.57%	6,450	43.72%
Season box seat rental	7,614	8.25%	6,091	12.69%	6,091	9.02%	761	5.79%	2,284	9.59%	2,284	7.86%	1,522	10.32%
Public funding	10,810	11.71%	8,648	18.02%	8,648	12.81%	1,081	8.22%	3,243	13.61%	3,243	11.16%	2,162	14.65%
Other income	3,366	3.65%	2,693	5.61%	2,693	3.99%	336	2.56%	1,009	4.24%	1,009	3.47%	673	4.56%
Operating costs	1,10,608		61,640		77,718		20,303		37,269		32,045		20,293	
Performances	10		8		8		1		3		3		2	
Cost per performance	11,061		7,705		9,715		20,303		12,423		10,682		10,147	
Orchestra	19,912	18.00%	7,314	11.87%	7,314	9.41%	914	4.50%	2,742	7.36%	2,742	8.56%	1,828	9.01%
Singers	51,925	46.95%	18,699	30.34%	36,935	47.52%	6,946	34.21%	18,814	50.48%	14,051	43.85%	7,393	36.43%
Conductors	7,441	6.73%	2,740	4.45%	2,740	3.53%	342	1.68%	1,027	2.76%	1,027	3.20%	685	3.38%
Choir	5,654	5.11%	4,523	7.34%	4,523	5.82%	565	2.78%	1,696	4.55%	1,696	5.29%	1,130	5.57%
Dancers & choreographer	0	0.00%	2,906	4.71%	0	0.00%	0	0.00%	0	0.00%	0	0.00%	726	3.58%
Scenery	3,366	3.04%	3,180	5.16%	807	1.04%	3,726	18.35%	1,382	3.71%	182	0.57%	121	0.60%
Copyright	4,000	3.62%	3,400	5.52%	4,000	5.15%	5,000	24.63%	4,000	10.73%	4,000	12.48%	2,000	9.86%
Services	18,310	16.55%	18,878	30.63%	21,399	27.53%	2,810	13.84%	7,608	20.41%	8,347	26.05%	6,410	31.59%

because, according to the firm, only full support of the industrial spirit of the collaboration could replace current losses with future profits. As Mocchi publicly explained: 'we must create the "repertoire theatre"', which would be based on three groups of productions that could 'circulate from Turin, to Rome, to Naples, every forty days', and 'in mid-April could be brought together with the orchestra, the chorus and the dancers of the Costanzi – all of whom would be engaged for five years in agreement with the Colón – to sail to Buenos Aires as a single company, with the repertoire all ready and prepared'.[104] Several years later, during World War I, Mocchi would realize his idea.

The STIN's financial difficulties were also causing problems for the publisher Sonzogno, its main shareholder. In an attempt to solve the enterprise's image problem, in 1909 Mocchi engaged Sonzogno's main composer, Pietro Mascagni (1863–1945), as general manager at the Teatro Costanzi. To accept the appointment, the composer had to stop working on his latest opera (see Figure 3.2). As he explained to his librettist, Luigi Illica: 'I should finish *Isabeau* (without instrumentation) by the end of November, because from December 1909 to October 15, 1911, I will be very busy in the Costanzi and in the Colon. That is why I'm writing furiously'.[105] From what he wrote to Illica, Mascagni was planning to remain at the Costanzi for two full seasons and end his tenure with the festivities commemorating the fiftieth anniversary of the unification of Italy. His time at the Costanzi, though, lasted only one season, 1909–1910.

During his time at the Costanzi, Mascagni envisioned the creation of a single operatic season that would include both Italian and South American venues. He wanted to develop a sustainable model that could run for years and greatly benefit the reputation of the Costanzi. The project aimed to move 'the same workers from Rome to Buenos Aires, and I am sure that in a couple of years the Costanzi would become the first theatre in the world'.[106] Mascagni signed an agreement with the STIN to serve as 'general manager for staging and conducting in any kind of performance given at the Costanzi . . ., not performing in any other place, neither public nor private . . ., excepting the Lenten concerts at the Corea Hall'.[107]

In his report to the board of directors, Mocchi claimed that he had 'the idea of engaging the Maestro Mascagni', and explained that Mascagni 'was hired as representing the STIA . . . merely as conductor and stage director', not as a 'theatre manager with administrative functions, because in his quality of Artist he must

---

[104] 'Un colloquio con Walter Mocchi sul programma della Società teatrale Internazionale', *La Stampa*, 20 February 1909.

[105] M. Morini, R. Iovino, and A. Paloscia (eds.), *Epistolario* (Libreria Musicale Italiana, 1996), p. 309.

[106] Ibid.

[107] ASC, *STIN*, b. 3, fasc. 25, Contract between Alberto Marghieri and Pietro Mascagni, 5 August 1909.

Figure 3.2 Pietro Mascagni and Walter Mocchi during the production of
Isabeau (*Il Teatro Illustrato*).

always have by his side a moderator representing the Capital'.[108] Mascagni's
purpose was clear: he was to promote the artistic image of the STIN and its main
venues in close association with the operations of the STIA in South America.

Although Mascagni was only at the Costanzi for one season, it had a lasting
effect on him. In 1927, he recalled his experience 'as one of the most noble in
my life'.[109] Mascagni's partnership with Mocchi lasted until 1923, and as a
strong believer in the STIN's reforms, the composer-conductor kept his company shares until 1927, after the fascists took over the company. The STIN
relaunched Mascagni's composing and conducting careers with glorious interoceanic tours that included commissions of new operas for the Italian and South
American markets. Despite frequent arguments with Mocchi and Sonzogno, the
STIN offered the famed composer his first and only experience as a director of a
theatre, meaning that he had to be concerned with both artistic and managerial
matters. Mascagni had to coordinate his efforts with the Municipality of Rome
and STIN's board[110] and also deal with publishers. 'I had to parry the blow of

---

[108] ASCC, *TCP*, b. 710/1908, f. 4, *Verbale di Assemblea Generale di 2ª convocazione della
Anonima Società 'Teatrale Internazionale'*, 11 September 1909.

[109] ASCC, *TCP*, b. 710/1908, f. 29, *Verbale di assemblea ordinaria degli azionisti della Società
Teatrale Internazionale*, 24 February 1927.

[110] A large amount of correspondence and accounting ledgers survive that detail transactions
between Mascagni, the Municipality of Rome, and the STIN. Most of these documents are
now preserved in the Archivio Storico Capitolino and the Archivio della Camera di Commercio
of Rome.

Figure 3.3 Pietro Mascagni, 'The Tsar of the Costanzi' (*Ars et Labor*)

the new operas that Ricordi wanted to impose, *Ellera* [*sic*] and *Grillo del focolare* (The Cricket on the Hearth)', he recalled.[111] Ricordi posed a distinctive challenge, since it was the rival house to Mascagni's own publisher and the STIN's lead shareholder, Sonzogno. Ricordi's magazine, *Ars et Labor*, dedicated a long article, 'The Tsar of the Costanzi', to Mascagni's new appointment that moved from satire to admiration (see Figure 3.3):

> And here is Mascagni in his brand new functions of administrator, conductor, stage director, etc. etc., at the Costanzi Theatre of Rome; here is Mascagni on stage, while he supervises the refurbishment of the venue; he also became an architect, electrician, stage hand ... and we also hope *radiator technician*, since we remember in the hall some polar temperatures that could have sent Peary and Cook into raptures .... Even though we prefer a Pietro Mascagni who composes new scores, we wish all the best to the new Director of the

---

[111] M. Morini, R. Iovino, and A. Paloscia (eds.), *Epistolario ...*, p. 316.

Opera House of the Italian Capital City: his artistic purposes are beautiful, and can benefit the Italian art that we insist be put above all the others.[112]

Mascagni administered all aspects of the Costanzi. He had to develop the budget, deal with publishers' requests, discern audience tastes, hire an orchestra, and consider the real market possibilities for an art form that had lost money the previous season. Mascagni also had to deal with the reality that many Italian singers were fleeing to more lucrative foreign markets:

Given the current penury of artists that remain in Italy, as well as the absolute necessity of coordinating the repertoire with the few available artists, I dedicated all my humble activity to creating a season able to fulfil the modern requirements of Art, worthy of the major theatre of the Capital.[113]

If Mocchi's ultimate goal for placing Mascagni at the helm of the Costanzi was to increase the artistic reputation of the STIN, his plan was an unqualified success. Mascagni's main Carnival season balanced Italian and foreign works, new operas alongside past favourites. Sonzogno placed all his new operas in the season (Umberto Giordano's *Mese Mariano*, Giocondo Fino's *La festa del grano* (The Grain Festival) and Ruggero Leoncavallo's *Majà*), while Ricordi saw six out of the eleven operas that were staged, including Arrigo Boito's *Mefistofele*. Mascagni fulfilled his passion for Wagner by opening his tenure with *Tristan and Iseult*, whose lavish staging, 'for its beauty, seemed without any precedent',[114] and presenting *Lohengrin* later in the season. To ensure box-office receipts, the composer programmed some of Ricordi's bestsellers (Puccini's *La Bohème*, Bellini's *Norma*), as well as his own *Iris* and *Cavalleria rusticana*, twenty years after its glorious premiere at the Costanzi.[115] Perhaps the most significant event of the season was the rediscovery of Verdi's *Don Carlo,* which had never been seen at the Costanzi and was greeted as a huge success. Originally planned to play six nights, the grand opera ran for eleven, to become the most profitable title of the season.

The Costanzi company was impressive, to say the least. The cast included many of the stars signed to the STIA, endorsing the relationship between that company and the STIN. The principal singers included luminaries such as Emma Carelli, Giannina Russ, Maria Farneti, Giuseppe De Luca, Carlo Walter, and Ignazio Digas. The chorus included fifty male and thirty-six

---

[112] 'Lo czar del Teatro Costanzi in Roma', *Ars et Labor*, 15 November 1909.

[113] ASC, *X*, b. 54, f. 4, Letter of Pietro Mascagni to the Mayor of Rome, 3 November 1909.

[114] V. Frajese, *Dal Costanzi all'Opera: cronache, recensioni e documenti in 4 volumi* (Capitolium, 1977), vol. 2, p. 24.

[115] *Cavalleria rusticana* replaced Massenet's *Werther*, originally planned.

female singers, while Mascagni called the seventy-nine-member orchestra[116] 'extraordinary'.[117]

Mascagni began rehearsals for *Tristan and Iseult* on 25 November, three weeks before the season opened. The Maestro noted: 'The orchestra rehearsals proceed regularly day and night, without any incident [and] with great exuberance of good will from every single musician'.[118] Mascagni's work proceeded quickly. After one week, on 3 December, the Maestro noted that he was 'ready in the orchestra with *Tristan*, started to rehearse *Bohème*, and in the morning and at night he read the whole score; considering there was nothing more to be rehearsed, he ordered for the next day the rehearsal of *Mefistofele*'.[119] Mascagni's fast pace drew the attention of some critics, who noted: 'his commitments are huge . . ., but he has to study the scores during the rehearsals, and that is not acceptable!'[120] (In fact it was common practice.)

Mascagni's total commitment to the rehearsal process demanded discipline from the entire ensemble. The Maestro required the presence of every single player at every rehearsal, even when that person's part was not required. This practice was considered uncommon and obviously caused some troubles between Mascagni and the players. The conductor did not even consider what nowadays would be defined as 'union requests'. For example, when the chorus members demanded a 'weekly day of rest', the conductor replied 'that the chorus had an agreement that did not mention any free day', and 'the chorus members had very limited rehearsal time, so the request was declined'.[121] Although the performers did not appreciate this ruthless attitude, the STIN's board did and expected it to result in 'a triumph both of [artistic] fulfilment and box office [receipts]'.[122] Mascagni met their expectations, and the season closed with an impressive profit of L. 117,144.63.[123] As would be expected, familiar operas made more money than new ones (see Table 3.3).

The success of the Carnival season inspired Mascagni to plan a grand programme for the 1911 celebration of the unification of Italy. Enrico di San Martino, president of the STIN, was in charge of the event and did not want any competition from Mascagni. So, on 28 January 1910, during the Carnival season, the STIN board formalized an agreement that gave control of the

[116] The detailed list of the orchestra members, including payrolls, can be found in ASC, *STIN*, b. 16, f. 7.

[117] ASC, *STIN*, b. 4, f. 15, *Stagione lirica 1909–10. Foglio di appunti no. 1.*   [118] Ibid.

[119] ASC, *STIN*, b. 4, f. 15, *Stagione lirica 1909–10. Foglio di appunti no. 2.*

[120] 'Dalla Capitale. Mascagni al Costanzi', *Il Teatro Illustrato*, 1–15 February 1910.

[121] ASC, *STIN*, b. 16, f. 7, *Stagione lirica 1909–10. Foglio di appunti no. 2.*

[122] ASC, *STIN*, b. 4, f. 15, Letter from Roberto De Sanna to Pietro Mascagni, 10 December 1909.

[123] ASC, *STIN*, b. 5, f. 1, *Copia pubblica del Verbale di Assemblea generale degli azionisti della Società Teatrale Internazionale del 26 settembre 1910.*

Table 3.3 Revenues of Mascagni's managing season at the Costanzi (1909–1910). Author's elaboration on STIN's financial statements (ASC, *STIN*, b. 34, f. 3)

Opera	Don Carlo	La Bohème	Mefistofele	Lohengrin	Il Barbiere di Siviglia	Veglione impero (masked ball)	Tristan and Iseult	Norma	Iris	Majà	La Festa del grano	Mese Mariano / Cavalleria rusticana
Performances	11	12	12	8	1	1	6	10	10	5	4	4
Revenues	78,509	54,384	58,398	42,333	5,000	5,539	23,139	42,630	41,061	10,986	6,044	18,759
Revenues per night	7,137	4,532	4,866	5,291	5,000	5,539	3,856	4,263	4,106	2,197	1,601	4,689

1911 celebrations at the Costanzi to a committee that San Martino would chair.[124] Mascagni strongly protested and threatened to resign. The rival publishers Ricordi[125] and Sonzogno banded together and forced Mascagni to remain, warning him of 'the madness of your resignation, that may cause a disaster of which you will assume the huge and full responsibility'.[126] The season came to its natural end, as a success, and Sonzogno pressured Mascagni to get back to work on *Isabeau*.

The STIN constituted another career-defining milestone for Mocchi. Modelling the Società (STIN) on the Sociedad (STIA) and forging a symbiotic relationship between the two organizations, he established a transatlantic cooperative that sat firmly in place as the twentieth century entered its second decade. Through the STIN, Mocchi discovered creative solutions to the financial dilemmas engulfing the Italian theatre industry, namely mounting lucrative operetta seasons and promoting high-profile celebrities such as Mascagni. In order to maximize the effectiveness of such innovations in a transoceanic marketplace, a new company would be needed. Mocchi thus founded La Teatral, a new entity that synthesized best practice from the STIA, through its network concept, with that of the STIN, with its overt promotion of star power and operetta.

4. Becoming the 'Buffalo Bill of Italian Impresarios': Mocchi and La Teatral

In early 1910, the two theatrical trusts based on either side of the Atlantic, the Socied Teatral Ítalo-Argentina (STIA) and the Società Teatrale Internazionale (STIN), redefined their relationship. This negotiation did not take place on friendly terms. Through a complex and shady transfer of shares and voting stakes the STIA managed to gain full control of the STIN.[127] Playing a major role in the takeover were the STIA's main shareholders, Charles Séguin and Edorardo Sonzogno, and of course, Walter Mocchi. With the support of Séguin and Sonzogno, Mocchi then established a new company, La Teatral, partly to take over the activities of both the STIA and STIN. When Mocchi and Luigi Ducci founded La Teatral in Buenos Aires's Coliseo Theatre in December 1909,[128] they chose the legal form of a limited partnership, which allowed

---

[124] The agreement is not preserved in the corporate archive. However, it is described in detail in a surviving document. ASC, *STIN*, b. 4, f. 16.

[125] ASC, *STIN*, b. 4, f. 15, Telegram from Giulio Ricordi to Pietro Mascagni, 11 February 1910.

[126] ASC, *STIN*, b. 4, f. 15, Telegram from Renzo Sonzogno to Pietro Mascagni, 12 February 1910.

[127] For a detailed discussion of the STIN's corporate evolution, see M. Paoletti, *Mascagni, Mocchi, Sonzogno. La Società Teatrale Internazionale (1908–1931) e i suoi protagonisti* (Alma Mater Studiorum Bologna, 2015), https://doi.org/10.6092/unibo/amsacta/4235, pp. 216–48, 268–74.

[128] 'La Teatrale', *Il Teatro Illustrato*, 1–15 January 1910.

them to control corporate activity in an easier and faster way than through the joint-stock model. Mocchi, now at the helm of La Teatral, the STIA, and the STIN, could personally oversee the entire theatrical enterprise with the aid of a few secondary associates. La Teatral's South American holdings included the Coliseo in Buenos Aires, the Municipal in Santiago de Chile, the São José in São Paulo, and multiple smaller venues. In 1914 Mocchi regained control of the Colón in partnership with Faustino da Rosa, adding to his power. To strengthen his presence in the Italian market, the impresario established a new agency in Milan, the Agenzia Teatrale Italo-Sud-Americana, to provide artists and performance materials for his South American tours.[129] Years later Mascagni dubbed Mocchi the 'Buffalo Bill of Italian impresarios abroad', referring to his somewhat renegade commercial and populist reputation.[130] Mocchi, through La Teatral, continued to distinguish himself through his three most distinctive projects: operetta, Mascagni, and the Costanzi Theatre in Rome.

Operetta maintained its prominent role in Mocchi's coordinated transatlantic seasons. La Teatral held exclusive rights to the Scognamiglio–Caramba Company (see Figure 4.1),[131] which along with the Giulio Marchetti Company, now the property of La Teatral, realized the potential of the transatlantic operetta market. In April 1910 the Giulio Marchetti Company sailed from Genoa to Buenos Aires, and after a South American tour lasting nearly eleven months, returned to Italy to play at the Costanzi in Rome, the Teatro Giacosa in Naples, and the Chiarella in Turin.[132] The box-office success of this demanding schedule inspired Mocchi to keep the Giulio Marchetti Company on a never-ending tour. The troupe continued to tour South America for most of the main Italian season and during the southern hemisphere's winter months (summertime in the northern hemisphere). It would return to Italy for brief annual visits some time in February or March, then go back to South America.

Operetta continued to draw large audiences and bring in more money than other offerings. During the 1910–1911 season dramatic offerings at the Costanzi by two of the major Italian companies, Ferruccio Garavaglia and Ermete

---

[129] The company was established in Milan on 15 October 1910, and its seat was in via San Pietro all'Orto 7, in the premises of *Il Teatro Illustrato*. Its corporate purpose was 'The engagement of artists as brokerage company', and its duration was set at ten years. The company was wound up on 25 March 1920. Archivio Storico della Camera di Commercio di Milano, *Sezione X^ (Registro ditte) – Notifiche e iscrizioni ditte (1853–1920)*, b. 395, f. 2, *Denuncia di Costituzione di Società in Accomandita Semplice*, 27 May 1911.

[130] 'Mascagni e Walter Mocchi alle mani', *La Stampa*, 15 March 1923. Buffalo Bill (William Frederick Cody, 1846–1917) was an American showman who popularized the American West through his travelling show, 'Buffalo Bill's Wild West'.

[131] All the contracts are preserved in ASC, *STIN*, b. 4, f. 4

[132] ASC, *STIN*, b. 8, f. 8, Letter from Renzo Sonzogno to Enrico di San Martino, 8 January 1909.

Zacconi, brought profits of L. 2.477,05 and 6.812,08, while operetta performances by the Giulio Marchetti and Scognamiglio–Caramba companies earned far more than double the combined income of the two dramatic seasons, L. 15.739,45 for Giulio Marchetti and L. 19.089,65 for Scognamiglio–Caramba. The latter company's greatest successes that season were three operettas new to Rome: Mario Costa's *Il Capitan Fracassa* (Captain Fracassa), Franz Lehár's *La Figlia del Brigante* (Das Fürstenkind), and Leo Fall's *La Principessa dei Dollari* (Die Dollaprinzessin).[133]

Indeed, the success of operetta, as seen in the previous section, helped impresarios such as Mocchi counteract poor revenues from their opera and spoken-drama seasons. The municipal authorities that provided grants to theatres considered operetta 'commercial speculation' and refused to give money to support the wildly popular genre. Hence, many producers, including La Teatral, continued to give up municipal grants with the knowledge that they would earn more money by not accepting the grant and instead mounting operettas. Renzo Sonzogno spoke the truth when he said that operetta could now really replace opera in the main opera houses.[134]

Mocchi's entrepreneurial spirit when it came to operetta found an unexpected outlet in 1913 when a new operetta appeared at his Coliseo Theatre in Buenos Aires, one that featured a caricature of Mocchi himself. The Scognamiglio–Caramba Company's production of *13* by Vincenzo Di Napoli-Vita took as its subject the fight between famous impresarios to take control of the South American market. The winner in the story, of course, is La Teatral.[135] The operetta testifies that Mocchi was not alone in his endeavour but was the most significant.[136]

Late in 1913 the Scognamiglio–Caramba and the Giulio Marchetti companies merged to become the Compagnia Italiana d'Opera Comica (Italian Company of Comic Opera). La Teatral, which owned the new company, forced the merger, since it was more cost effective to run one operetta company than two. The new company's main singers included Tina Ghirelli, Maria Ivanisi, Giulia Bassi, Janka Chaplinska, and Giuseppe Zoffoli. Edoardo Buccini and

---

[133] ASCC, *TCP*, b. 710/1908, f. 7, *Verbale di Assemblea generale ordinaria degli azionisti della Società Teatrale Internazionale*, 21 December 1911.

[134] 'The Scognamiglio-Caramba Company ... is the only one that may decently replace the Carnival opera season'. ASC, *STIN*, b. 4, f. 4, Letter from Renzo Sonzogno to Alberto Marghieri, 21 February 1910.

[135] The production team included the costume designer Caramba, the writer Carlo Vizzotto, the conductor Vincenzo Bellezza, the producer Giulio Marchetti, and other members of the Argentine cultural community. See J. I. Weber, L. Martinovich, and P. Camerata, 'Itinerari di compagnie liriche italiane attraverso le città del litorale fluviale argentino (1908–1910)', in A. E. Cetrangolo and M. Paoletti (eds.), *I fiumi che cantano. L'opera italiana nel bacino del Rio de la Plata* (Alma Mater Studiorum Bologna, 2020).

[136] Among Mocchi's competitors were Luigi Carpentiero, João Cateysson, and Achille Del Puente.

Figure 4.1 The Scognamiglio–Caramba Company on stage at the Costanzi
(1910). (*Il Teatro illustrato*)

Vincenzo Bellezza (1888–1964), who later became the main conductor for
Mocchi's opera seasons, served as its conductors.

The second of Mocchi's projects concerned the career of Pietro Mascagni. The
relationship between Mascagni, Mocchi, and San Martino remained tense after
Mascagni left the Costanzi. San Martino pushed Mascagni to the sidelines when
the composer-conductor seemed to be creating competition for San Martino's
plans for the 1911 celebrations for the anniversary of the unification of Italy.
Mocchi, though, wanted to make amends with Mascagniand actually help him
take revenge on San Martino. He did this by arranging to have the premiere of his
Mascagni's opera *Isabeau* take place not in Italy but in Argentina.

The initial plan was for *Isabeau* to open in Rome, especially because of the
massive flow of public funding going to the capital for the 1911 festivities.
Rome's mayor, Ernesto Nathan, pressed Mascagni to give the premiere in his
city in order 'to increase the solemnity and entirety of the Italian art in such a
memorable year for Rome and the Homeland'.[137] Wanting to avenge himself on
San Martino, Mascagni replied that he 'could guarantee the performance in
Rome by mid-April, before leaving for South America, on the sole condition . . .
[that it be produced by] an organization completely independent from the
Committee'.[138] Mascagni's condition was not accepted, and no opera by
Mascagni was performed during the celebrations.

Mocchi wanted the premiere of *Isabeau* to get as much attention as possible, so
he promoted the opera through an aggressive and unceasing press campaign that
involved his own magazine, *Il Teatro illustrato*, as well as the major Italian and
Argentine newspapers. The impresario displayed tremendous generosity (e.g. in

---

[137] ASC, *X*, b. 54, f. 5, Telegram from Ernesto Nathan to Pietro Mascagni, 22 February 1911.
[138] ASC, *X*, b. 54, f. 5, Telegram from Pietro Mascagni to Ernesto Nathan, 23 February 1911.

terms of marketing) by granting many interviews, gossipy remarks, and 'unofficial' leaks to multiple media outlets. He wanted to ensure that the opera's debut on 2 June 1911 at the Coliseo in Buenos Aires would garner the attention it deserved. This was, after all, the first time that a living European composer of such importance had had a world premiere take place in South America. Before the cast boarded the liner *Tommaso di Savoia* in Genoa on 10 April 1911, a press preview of *Isabeau* took place at the Carlo Felice opera house. It was a concert performance, without the captivating scenery of Antonio Rovescalli or the sumptuous costumes of Adolf Hohenstein and Caramba, and was put on with the express purpose of introducing the score to Italian critics.[139]

Thousands of people were waiting on the wharf in Buenos Aires when the liner arrived on 2 May 1911, and Mascagni became the object of true worship: 'the delirious crowd attempted many times to hoist the Maestro on their arms', reported one popular Argentine magazine, 'however Mascagni declined such an uncomfortable honour'.[140] Mascagni himself conducted the premiere, which was hailed as 'an historical event' and praised by 'unanimous ovations ... of a huge audience that admired the presence of the famed composer and the staging of his creation'.[141] *Isabeau* and Mascagni were not just welcomed but feted throughout their tour of South America.[142] Following its South American triumph the opera was performed in Italy at Teatro alla Scala and at the Costanzi. Despite the opera's success (or perhaps because of it), the publisher Sonzogno accused Mocchi of not paying him all the royalties due him from the South American tour. This started a legal trial that became a press sensation, and which La Teatral won.[143]

In addition to operetta and Mascagni, Mocchi also scored success with the management of the Costanzi in Rome. Much of this was due to the efforts of his wife, Emma Carelli, who had taken on managerial responsibilities at the theatre. On December 1911, La Teatral signed an agreement with the STIN to run the Costanzi through the 1913–1914 Carnival season for a fixed lease of L. 100,000 per year and 10 per cent of the gross income. La Teatral's first Carnival season at the Costanzi, conducted by Edoardo Vitale, provided natural continuity from the just-completed South American season, since the operas and the casts were nearly identical. Mocchi's recently established Agenzia Teatrale Italo-Sud-Americana handled all the contracts for the Italian performances, just as it had

---

[139] Correspondence between Mocchi and the Municipality in Archivio Storico Comunale of Genova, *Amministrazione Comunale 1860–1910*, b. 1002 [30], f. 3.

[140] *Caras y Caretas*, 6 May 1911.   [141] *Caras y Caretas*, 10 June 1911.

[142] M. Morini, R. Iovino, and A. Paloscia (eds.), *Epistolario ...*, pp. 336–45.

[143] 'Sentenza favorevole alla "Teatral" nella causa contro la Casa Musicale Edoardo Sonzogno', *Il Teatro Illustrato*, 29 February 1912.

for the South American ones.[144] Many of these titles belonged to the catalogue of Lorenzo (Renzo) Sonzogno's brand-new publishing company, which he had established in direct competition to that of his uncle Edoardo and cousin Riccardo.[145] Mocchi, as a sharp businessman, was able to keep good working relations with both branches of the feuding Sonzogno family.

Of the season's offerings, perhaps the most significant was the Roman premiere of Richard Strauss's highly controversial *Elektra*, which ran at the Costanzi from 7 February to 13 April 1912. Emma Carelli's performance in the title role was described as 'one of the most genius-inspired and complete in the theatrical world', 'beyond any commendation', an 'artistic miracle', in reviews that described her as someone who 'seemed to be willing to forget that she was a distinguished and gifted artist who had not sung for almost two years, [instead] dedicating all the passion of her rich nature to the humble, unappreciated work of theatrical management'.[146]

Mocchi, meanwhile, faced new challenges from Ernesto Nathan, the mayor of Rome. As was typical for Mocchi, he once again managed to convince an opponent to take his point of view. While the impresario was in South America, Nathan had denied public funding to the Costanzi for the 1911–1912 season, claiming that a 'manifest and unjustified disproportion' of the total grant funding went to opera as compared to the other arts.[147] (The Costanzi did not promote operetta during its main seasons at the time, so it could apply for grants.) The funding of the Costanzi became an ideological battleground for a political debate on public–private partnerships. While Mocchi was abroad, Emma Carelli started negotiations with the mayor regarding the annual L. 80,000 grant for the opera season. She justified her request by stating that this funding was 'the usual practice of the main cities, including Rome' and was especially important this year because of the 'difficult conditions of the operatic market after the long 1911

---

[144] Repertory included *Siegfried*, which opened the season, *La Traviata*, *La Wally* (by Alfredo Catalani and Luigi Illica), *Lucia di Lammermoor*, *La Bohème*, *L'Africaine*, *Un ballo in maschera*, *Linda di Chamounix* (by Donizetti and Gaetano Rossi), *La Fanciulla del West*, and three operas that were new to Rome: Riccardo Zandonai's *Conchita*, Engelbert Humperdinck's *Figli di Re* (Sons of Kings), and Richard Strauss's *Elektra*.

[145] Due to arguments with Edoardo Sonzogno, in 1911 Edoardo's nephew Lorenzo (Renzo) established a competing publishing company, while Riccardo kept on managing his uncle's musical division. (Riccardo was the son of Edoardo's brother, Alberto.) Renzo purchased exclusive Italian rights for many works by Ermanno Wolf-Ferrari, Engelbert Humperdinck, Alberto Franchetti, Richard Strauss, and Nikolai Rimsky-Korsakov. He also published the poetry of the prominent Italian poet Gabriele d'Annunzio (1863–1938). Mascagni moved to the new company at Mocchi's suggestion. In July 1915, the sudden death of Riccardo led Edoardo and Renzo to reconcile, merge their catalogues, and establish the new Casa Musicale Sonzogno.

[146] *La Vita*, 8 February 1912. The previous quotations were from *Corriere d'Italia* and *La Tribuna*. Wide press review in Frajese, *Dal Costanzi all'opera . . .*, pp. 62–3.

[147] ASC, *X*, b. 55, f. 3, *Verbale delle Deliberazioni della Giunta Municipale di Roma – Seduta del giorno 30 dicembre 1911 – Estratto n. 142.*

Celebrations, which had exhausted the audience and increased the demands of the artists, who became used to the exceptional salaries that only the Committee could afford, thus creating an unsustainable precedent'.[148] Mocchi, who after all had been a socialist politician, exploited the controversy to his own advantage after his return from South America. The responsibility of the mayor, he proclaimed, should 'not [be to provide] the mere subsidy of a patron, but the development of a regular agreement between [Mocchi's] company and the Municipality that could offer in return the benefits of a real business partnership' that would profit not the wealthy but rather the Italian public:

> I consider it superfluous to continue the debate regarding *sovvenzioni teatrali* (theatrical grants), once considered unproductive or luxurious liabilities, or even worse a means to provide the wealthy classes relatively cheap shows through public funding. Most of the popular, republican and socialist administrations of Northern Italy have already provided grants to their theatres, thus clearly demonstrating the abolition of the theatrical privilege of the wealthy classes through the economic development of the *classi lavoratrici* [working classes] and the instigation of performances at popular [lower] prices. Everywhere operas are no longer considered entertainment but true aesthetic education that is essential for our country. ... Therefore, my company is ready to take on clearly stated honours and duties and is asking the Municipality for sufficient, if not sumptuous, financial support that has to continue in order to plan realistically the next three seasons.[149]

Mocchi's consummate appeal worked. The former politician leveraged civic responsibility, access to opera, and the importance of opera as part of an essential national agenda in order to receive the annual L. 80,000 subsidy for the next three seasons (1911–1914). As its part of the agreement, La Teatral needed to continue its existing practice of offering popular operas at modest prices and to stage every year 'a revival of a classic nature, and at least one new work'.[150] Moreover, the company had to prioritize Roman musicians for its orchestra and choir and 'ensure their employment when the Costanzi is closed, providing jobs for most of them on the South American tours'.[151] The subsidy and agreement were finalized on 6 March.[152]

Mocchi and Carelli were often accused of adhering formally to contracts on paper while actually behaving in somewhat shady ways. One observer noted:

---

[148] ASC, *X*, b. 55, f. 3, Letter from Emma Carelli to Ernesto Nathan, 2 November 1911.

[149] ASC, *X*, b. 55, f. 3, Letter from Walter Mocchi to Ernesto Nathan, 15 December 1911.

[150] ASC, *X*, b. 56, f. 1, *Copia del contratto tra il Comune di Roma e l'Impresa del Teatro Costanzi*, 25 March 1912.

[151] ASC, *X*, b. 55, f. 3, *Verbale di deliberazione della Giunta Municipale di Roma – Seduta del 24 gennaio 1912.*

[152] ASC, *X*, b. 56, f. 1, *Copia del contratto tra il Comune di Roma e l'Impresa del Teatro Costanzi*, 25 March 1912.

I would like to learn from the Municipality what kind of *fregatura* (swindle) takes place during the popular runs at the Costanzi .... The money from the [municipal] grant now goes to an impresario who makes good money giving comfortable seats to fat bourgeois or noble subscribers. What happens on the few Sundays when a poor man sees the fateful motto 'popular prices' appearing on the billboard? He rushes with his Lira in his hand at 3.30 p. m., two hours before the show, and finds no place for him. Everything is already taken: the centre stalls are for the numbered tickets, the second tier the same, the third the same, the fourth the same. There are just a few scrap seats left, where the wretched people of Rome – and also some foreigners – *si pigia pestandosi i calli* [must scratch each other's toes] and quarrel continuously, ... climb over the seats and move all the time to step around the column or over the hat of their neighbour.[153]

Despite its controversies the Costanzi was a profit-generating venue. After its Carnival season ended in 1912, the Costanzi company boarded the liner *Principe di Udine* in Genoa (see Figure 4.2) and headed for South America as proof of 'the overseas triumphs of the whole complex and large exploitation of La Teatral'.[154] Conducted by Gino Marinuzzi, the Roman company toured extensively in Chile, Argentina, Uruguay, and Brazil.[155] The company did not include *Elektra* in its tour repertoire since its star, Emma Carelli, remained in Italy.

Carelli was involved with running theatres in the years leading up to her triumph in *Elektra*, and after this success, she largely gave up her performing career to focus on her increasingly demanding work as an impresario.[156] With her husband spending so much time in South America, it became useful for her to remain in Rome as an active presence in the daily operations of the Costanzi. Carelli controlled all activity at the Costanzi until 1926, making her one of the most powerful and controversial women in Italy sometimes satirized in the press (see Figure 4.3).

---

[153] ASC, *X*, b. 55, f. 4, Anonymous letter to the City Council of Rome [7 February 1912].

[154] 'La grande "tournée" lirica della "Teatral" nel Sud-America', *Il Teatro Illustrato*, 15 April 1912.

[155] The cast included Ersilde Cervi-Caroli, Rosina Storchio, Maria Marek, Gilda Flory, Elena Rakowska, Luigi Marini, Renzo Minolfi, Gualtiero Favi, Giuseppe Taccani, Cesare Spadoni, Ettore Trucchi-Dorini, Paolo Argentini, Giulio Cirino, and Giorgio Schottler. The Costanzi's choreographer, Romeo Francioli, was credited in South America as 'regisseur-coreografo' (director-choreographer), a somewhat unusual designation for the time.

[156] Carelli did not completely abandon the operatic stage. Before reprising the title role in *Elektra* in South America in 1914, in 1912 she accepted an invitation from Gabriele d'Annunzio and Ildebrando Pizzetti to perform the title role in their new opera *Fedra*, which Lorenzo Sonzogno was producing as an overt attack on the two major publishers at the time, his uncle Edoardo and Ricordi. Mocchi included the premiere of *Fedra* in a list of repertoire planned for the upcoming season in a proposal presented to the Municipality of Rome, featuring his wife in the leading role. (ASC, *X*, b. 55, f. 4, Letter from Walter Mocchi to Alberto Tonelli, 31 October 1912.) The performance of *Fedra* at the Costanzi did not materialize, and the opera had its premiere on 20 March 1915, at Teatro alla Scala with Salomea Krusceniski, a singer under contract to Mocchi, in the title role.

Figure 4.2 La Teatral's company boarding the liner *Principe di Udine* in Genoa in April 1912. In the centre, the publisher Edoardo Sonzogno between Hariclea Darclée (left) and Emma Carelli (right) (*Il Teatro Illustrato*)

Avvenimenti teatrali del giorno

La nuova direttrice generale della « Teatral », Emma Carelli, ascolta in audizione il distinto tenore Walter Mocchi.

Figure 4.3 Luigi Ricordi's magazine *L'Arte Lirica* satirized Mocchi and Carelli's power. The picture describes 'The new general manager of the Teatral, Emma Carelli, who is auditioning the distinct tenor Walter Mocchi', while Pietro Mascagni watches from behind the door (*L'Arte Lirica*, 16 July 1911)

Not long after the Carnival season ended in 1912 and the Costanzi troupe departed for South America, Carelli produced a short season of operetta with the renowned Città di Milano beginning on 20 April, shortly before that company, like others associated with Mocchi, departed for South America. Conducted by Enrico Valle, the company performed Franz Lehár's *Eva* and *Amor di Zingaro* (Gipsy Love) and gave the premiere of Ruggero Leoncavallo's *La Reginetta delle rose* (Queen of the Roses). Carelli also offered special events at the Costanzi in the late spring, including two performances featuring Isadore Duncan, one of the founders of modern dance, in a program of dances and choruses from Gluck's *Iphigenie* that was performed on 22 and 25 April 1912. Carelli kept the theatre closed from 9 July to 25 October, since the resident company was in South America, and reopened it with a residency by Ermete Zacconi's theatre company.

With the return of the Costanzi company from South America, the 1912–1913 Carnival season began on 26 December. The season was extraordinarily rich: between 26 December 1912 and 17 April 1913, the Costanzi was open for an astonishing ninety-eight nights. Among the highlights was the Roman premiere of Mascagni's *Isabeau* (6 February 1913), which ran for nineteen performances, and an exhibition of Futurist painters and sculptors that culminated in a conference on the influential Italian Futurist Umberto Boccioni (26 February) and in two 'Futurist nights' (22 February and 6 March).

The intense schedule was not without its opponents, particularly the performers themselves. The 'victims of the orchestra' protested against Carelli, claiming that she 'treats her employees as beasts', and shows 'no respect for either the old or the young, who need their jobs and subject themselves to her will and resignedly bear her maltreatment and tortures'.[157] In January sixteen members of the band at the Costanzi who were not part of the agreement with the municipality threatened to strike for better working conditions. The former socialist leader Mocchi proposed a raise of the minimum wage (from L. 1.85 to 2.20 for the rehearsals and from 3.50 to 4.50 for the evening performances), but when the musicians refused, he simply replaced them with sixteen new players. The protest caused a great deal of controversy in the press and in the city council, but the impresario defended himself on the normalcy of his action.[158]

The Carnival season of 1913–1914 was the last one in which La Teatral directly ran the Costanzi. Beginning in 1914, Impresa Teatro Costanzi, a new enterprise specifically created by Mocchi and Carelli, managed the Roman opera house, which was still formally the property of the STIN. La Teatral's

---

[157] ASC, *X*, b. 55, f. 4, Anonymous letter to the City Council of Rome [4 April 1913].

[158] 'Il grave dissidio fra i bandisti del Costanzi e l'Impresa. Ciò che dice Walter Mocchi', *Giornale d'Italia*, 13 January 1913.

final season included three especially noteworthy events: the Italian premiere of Wagner's *Parsifal* on 1 January 1914, the premiere of Gianfrancesco Malipiero's *Canossa* on 24 January, and the Roman debut of Mascagni-d'Annunzio's opera *Parisina* on 21 March.[159] The season continued the impressive number of productions characteristic of La Teatral: 100 nights in three-and-a-half months, 22 of which were *Parsifal*. The obligatory South American tour followed. Conducted by Edoardo Vitale, in Argentina and Brazil the company performed *Parsifal* and *Parisina*, *Elektra* with Carelli returning to the role, and a lavish production of *Isabeau* with the famed singers Rosina Storchio, Tito Schipa, Mario Sammarco, and Maria Farneti. As in the past, most of the performers were from the Costanzi: seventy musicians in the orchestra, sixty in the chorus, twenty-four dancers, and twenty band players.[160] While the company was sailing to Buenos Aires on April 1914, Mocchi was already anticipating their return and advertising the next Carnival season at the Costanzi.[161]

5. Mocchi and World War I: New Challenges, New Cooperations

While the Costanzi company was travelling in South America during the European summer of 1914, tragedy struck. On 28 June, the assassination of Archduke Franz Ferdinand of Austria ignited World War I, a conflict that would have far-reaching consequences, including for Mocchi. Even though Italy remained neutral until 23 May 1915, the conflict had an immediately impact on the Italian theatrical world and caused a sudden shutdown of theatres and agencies.[162] 'I can't even hope to find anywhere to conduct, because the theatres are not open anymore', wrote Mascagni, who declared himself 'destroyed because of the publishers that can no longer pay'.[163]

---

[159] *Parisina* made it to the stage after several tumultuous years filled with conflicts between the producer Mocchi, the publisher Renzo Sonzogno, the composer Mascagni, and the librettist Gabriele d'Annunzio. Sonzogno wanted Mascagni to work with d'Annunzio on *Parisina*, after Alberto Franchetti and Giacomo Puccini had both turned it down. In April 1912 Mascagni accepted the task and completed the first part of the opera in only four months. The excessive length of the libretto stopped his progress and, amidst controversy, some of it was cut. After the opera's premiere at La Scala on 15 December 1913, *Parisina* was shortened and d'Annunzio threatened to sue until a revised version debuted at the Costanzi. Sonzogno accused Mascagni of causing heavy financial losses to his company. See: C. Orselli, *Pietro Mascagni* (L'Epos, 2011), pp. 91–5, 269–83.

[160] In Italian theatres band players are hired to play parts on stage or backstage (e.g. in *La Traviata*, act I; *Rigoletto*, act I); these musicians have different contracts and union protection from the members of the orchestra, who always play in the pit.

[161] 'Teatro Costanzi – Il cartellone nella prossima stagione 1914–15', *Il Teatro Illustrato*, 15–30 April 1914.

[162] I. Piazzoni, *Dal "Teatro dei palchettisti' all'Ente autonomo*, pp. 196–200.

[163] M. Morini, R. Iovino, and A. Paloscia (eds.), *Epistolario . . .*, p. 16.

Carelli managed to organize the Carnival season, but some politicians accused her of 'using the war as a pretext to lower wages'.[164] On 26 December 1914, the season opened, as was the custom, with Wagner. This time it was *Götterdämmerung*. Other operas that season included *Thaïs*, *Il barbiere di Siviglia*, *La Gioconda*, *Faust*, *Tosca*, *La Fanciulla del West*, *L'Elisir d'amore*, *Aida*, and four new works: Riccardo Zandonai's *Francesca da Rimini*, Mario Mariotti's *Una tragedia Fiorentina* (A Florentine Tragedy), Romano Romani's *Fedra*, and Alberto Nepomuceno's *Abul*. Nepomuceno (1864–1920) was a Brazilian composer, and this was Mocchi's first attempt to introduce a South American opera to Italian audiences. The war was paralysing the circulation of artists, municipal grants, and the public's desire to attend cultural events. By season's end the situation had reached a critical point, and the Costanzi, like its siblings, was forced to close. The manager of the Città di Milano wrote to the mayor about the crisis an the effect it was having:

> Today the difficult situation created by the war . . . is worsened more than ever by the necessary entry of our country into the conflict in order to defend its cherished interests, which forces me and my company to remain in Rome without any chance of work, since the Costanzi is closed due to the excessive expenses that the management cannot afford.[165]

Mocchi, as usual, thought of a solution that would benefit not only the opera economy but also himself. His idea was to expand his interoceanic trust by extending the usual circulation between the Costanzi and South America to bring in more major opera houses. Even before war broke out, he was trying in February 1914, through La Teatral, to obtain the municipal grant to run the Khedivial Theatre in Cairo, Egypt.[166] Although that project never materialized, his next effort did: a cooperative arrangement between the Teatro Colón and Milan's famed Teatro alla Scala under the auspices of La Teatral. In December 1914 Mocchi and Faustino da Rosa once again received the grant to operate the Colón[167] (which they ran exclusively until 1918[168]) since 'their offer guarantees the use of a protective artistic organization from one of the main stages of Europe, that is the Costanzi, [which provides an] indisputable advantage that ensures the same quality of the company and its presentations'.[169] Since the Costanzi was closed at the time, Mocchi brokered a deal with Uberto Visconti di

---

[164] ASC, *X*, b. 55, f. 5, *Estratto dal Verbale della Seduta del Consiglio del 4 dicembre 1914*.

[165] ASC, *X*, b. 55, f. 5, Letter from Dante Majeroni to the Mayor of Rome, 27 May 1915.

[166] ASC, *Ripartizione XV (Spettacoli pubblici, 1911–1921)*, b. 28, f. 1069, Letter from Walter Mocchi to the Royal Commissary of the Municipality of Rome, 23 February 1914.

[167] 'Il Teatro Colon concesso a Walter Mocchi', *Il Teatro Illustrato*, 15–31 December 1914.

[168] Caamaño, *La historia del Teatro Colón 1908–1968*, vol. III, pp. 77–8.

[169] ASC, *X*, b. 55, f. 3, Letter from Emma Carelli to Adolfo Apolloni, [24] February 1915.

Modrone (representing La Scala) and Da Rosa (representing the Colón) to create a formal relationship between the two theatres.

The project did not involve the Costanzi, at least not at first, probably to keep Visconti, the patron of La Scala, from becoming overly suspect of a dangerous deal with the shady king of the transatlantic opera trade. La Scala and the Costanzi did become connected, not directly, but through the Colón, since both theatres had agreements with the Buenos Aires house. The new relationship allowed the Costanzi to reopen its doors, and the three theatres became bound together in what was described as an 'artistic and industrial agreement between the Impresa Teatro Costanzi and the enterprise of the Colón':

> Through the first agreement, the enterprise of the Colón will provide 66 per cent of the cost for all new scenery that will be created from now, both at the Teatro alla Scala and the Colón, and it will hold the rights to use them at La Scala, the Colón and also the Costanzi in Rome, which will pay to the management of the Colón 33 per cent of the cost of each set .... The second agreement ... is a kind of alliance that also involves La Scala of Milan, through which we will obtain the best artists, ensuring them a career between the main theatres in Italy and the most important one in America.[170]

The agreement caused several problems for Visconti, who was accused of 'shaming the artistic integrity' of La Scala,[171] but the Municipality of Milan accepted the contract since Visconti 'guaranteed the absolute financial independence of the two theatres'.[172]

In April 1915 the *Gazzetta dei Teatri* announced the Colón's 'Great official lyrical season 1915', created 'in artistic cooperation with Scala of Milan'.[173] The season involved three of the greatest male stars of the time (Enrico Caruso, Titta Ruffo, and Mario Sammarco), while most of the other artists came from Mocchi's Agenzia Teatrale Italo-Sud-Americana (Bernardo De Muro, Hipolito Lazaro, Ernestina Poli Randaccio, Rosa Raisa, and Gilda Dalla Rizza). The tight connection between the two Italian theatres was underlined by the fact that production staff came from both houses. La Scala offered the conductor Gino Marinuzzi, the 'Regisseur Generale' (general stage director) Vittorio Mingardi, and the chorus master Enrico Romeo, while the Costanzi provided the stage director Romeo Francioli and the choreographer Augusto Francioli. The repertoire included an equal number of operas from Ricordi's and Sonzogno's catalogues and featured classics as well as new works for the Colón's audience (the latter included Richard Strauss's *Der Rosenkavalier*, Riccardo Zandonai's

---

[170] ASC, *X*, b. 55, f. 3, Letter from Emma Carelli to Adolfo Apolloni, 5 April 1915.
[171] *Avanti!*, 13 April 1915.
[172] I. Piazzoni, *Dal 'Teatro dei palchettisti' all'Ente autonomo*, p. 190.
[173] *Gazzetta dei Teatri*, 22 April 1915.

Francesca da Rimini, Alberto Franchetti's *Notte di Leggenda* (Night of Legend), Eduardo García-Mansilla's *Ivan*, and Jules Massenet's *Jongleur de Notre Dame* (The Juggler of Notre Dame)).[174] The South American season was indeed frantic: Mingardi conducted twenty operas and gave eighty-one performances over seventy-eight days, and Caruso, who was engaged for only ten nights, performed twenty-eight times, plus five additional times for charity.[175]

The success of the South American part of the combination brewed animosity toward La Teatral. Roman musicians were afraid of being replaced by less expensive players from Argentina, while the Milanese protested against the agreement forced on them by Mocchi that made them 'accept the contract for America, [which was] worth less than the contract with La Scala'.[176] The mayor of Milan, Emilio Caldara, asked Visconti for concrete guarantees, since he suspected that a 'real transfer of the grant, with the disturbing circumstances to our main Theatre – with its glorious traditions that do not show any signs of impairment – could become a tool for international speculation of Art'.[177] A few days later, the official program of La Scala was announced, one which shared a significant number of co-productions with the Colón. Visconti wrote Caldara:

> I wanted to wait for the publication of the program for La Scala and the remarks I gave to the audience, before answering your letter with more authority. Now I can calmly and coolly object to your insistence in confusing a merely internal technical agreement, which can obtain more efficient, varied, and continuative artistic results than the ones that can be obtained through the usual theatrical practice, with a shady, masked transfer of my granting the contract to someone else .... I have no obligation to the Municipality to privilege any group of choral singers or orchestra players; on the contrary, I have the full right to engage the co-workers whom I consider the most able to achieve the aim of the agreement itself – for which I am the sole responsible party – which is the artistic quality of the productions at La Scala .... It is absurd to think that the entire orchestra and 80 per cent of the choir considered this blackmail, when instead it represents the highest aspiration of every qualified professional, a resulting contract with the Colón and a tour in South America that adds about L. 5,000 to La Scala's modest payroll of L. 1,200.[178]

---

[174] The repertoire also included *Tannhäuser, Falstaff, Africaine, Hamlet, Aida, Carmen, Fanciulla del West, Iris, Tosca, Cavalleria rusticana, Pagliacci, Rigoletto, Gioconda, Faust*, and *Manon*.

[175] 'La grande stagione lirica al Teatro Colon di Buenos Ayres', *Gazzetta dei Teatri*, 23 September 1915.

[176] AVM, *AFVM*, b. H75, f. 4, Letter from Emilio Caldara to Uberto Visconti di Modrone, 22 November 1915.

[177] Ibid.

[178] AVM, *AFVM*, b. H75, f. 4, Letter from Uberto Visconti di Modrone to Emilio Caldara, 27 November 1915.

The mayor replied that he felt 'relieved' and had 'nothing more to say'.[179] Visconti reminded the mayor of a former practice among the players at La Scala, who used to sail overseas at the end of the Carnival season. In March 1908, for instance, Visconti refused to allow the STIN's future president, Enrico di San Martino, to stage Gabriele d'Annunzio's *La Nave* (The Ship) at La Scala because during the spring 'most of the artists, the chorus and most of the workers, once they had finished their commitment in the Theatre, left Milan, and most of them were already engaged for the season in Buenos Aires'.[180] The established practice became more stable and profitable through the agreement with Mocchi.

The 1915–1916 Carnival billboard at the Costanzi advertised the season as 'an artistic cooperation with the Theatres alla Scala of Milan and Colón of Buenos Aires'. The tight connection between the three venues was evident from the names of the singers who appeared on all three stages, including many who had previously sung in Buenos Aires and Milan, but not Rome, such as Rosina Storchio, Rosa Raisa, Alessandro Bonci, Aureliano Pertile, and Tito Schipa, as well as the conductor, Edoardo Vitale.

Despite the solid organization of the interoceanic combination, in the early months of 1916 the war severely curtailed the circulation of artists on ocean liners. Furthermore, theatres had to face the fact that many of their employees were being called up for military service. New theatrical crises loomed. Emma Carelli wrote in April:

> I wish I could keep the commitment to stage *Les Huguenots* …, but the difficulties that every day complicate the running of the season absolutely prevent me from doing so. The call to arms has forced me to continuously replace orchestra players and chorus members, thus delaying and hindering the complex preparation that the importance of the productions requires. The problem of the principal artists is more difficult than ever … : I hired the tenor José Palet – the only one able to sing the arduous role of Raoul – but he suddenly became unavailable because he preferred to stay in Spain, his homeland, rather than come to Italy, even for a few performances, in these difficult times.[181]

In response to the problems caused by the continuing war, Mocchi, Da Rosa, Carelli, and Visconti tightened their association, convinced that only a stable circulation of performers, including principal singers, as well as longer and

---

[179] AVM, *AFVM*, b. H75, f. 4, Letter from Emilio Caldara to Uberto Visconti di Modrone, 13 December 1915.

[180] AVM, *AFVM*, b. H71, f. 7, Letter from Uberto Visconti di Modrone to Enrico di San Martino, 25 March 1908.

[181] ASC, *X*, b. 56, f. 1, Letter from Emma Carelli to Prospero Colonna, 27 March 1916.

coordinated contractual agreements, could guarantee a regular series of productions in such difficult times. While Mocchi was in South America planning the seasons for Rio's Teatro Municipal, Carelli was arranging contracts for the upcoming seasons at the Costanzi and La Scala, mostly for the chorus and supernumeraries.[182] She noted the importance of La Scala's contribution in a letter to Visconti's attorney, Paolo Bruzzi:

> I demand your consent to the condition that Mr Walter Mocchi made through me so that the contract between the Duke Visconti di Modrone and him regarding the 'entente' Scala–Colón could remain in effect. And precisely: La Scala must keep the commitment of providing the Colón with the orchestra and chorus, complete, without a single substitution, if this is not followed, I will be forced to invoke the contract, as attorney for Mr Walter Mocchi.[183]

La Scala replied that understanding and mutual assistance were necessary 'to form the orchestra and chorus in accordance with the needs of the two theatres'.[184] This consolidation caused tremendous outcries, among them the socialist party in Milan publicly accusing the Duke of a 'merger with the Colón of Buenos Aires [that] offends the dignity of La Scala'.[185]

Conductors played especially important roles in how the cooperation between La Scala and the Colón developed. The first artist Mocchi hired was the conductor and composer Hector Panizza (1875–1967). The influential conductor's contract bound him to both La Scala and the Colón, and he garnered tremendous success at both houses. Another La Scala conductor, the legendary Arturo Toscanini (1867–1957), by contrast, was responsible for the most violent attacks on the Duke's decision to enter into a partnership with Mocchi's domain. (Earlier, Mocchi had asked Toscanini to manage the interoceanic combination. He declined. See Figure 5.1) The Maestro considered the agreement between La Scala and the Colón to be a betrayal of the cultural ideals and artistic mission of the most important theatrical institution in the world, and the presence of the shifty Mocchi was an unbearable offence. Toscanini, in a letter to Visconti di Modrone that Toscanini's biographer Harvey Sachs calls 'probably the longest message he had ever written',[186] protested against the Duke's actions as

> violating a noble tradition of high moral significance, well established for years at La Scala, rooted in the conscience of the public and of the entire

---

[182] AVM, *AFVM*, b. H71, f. 9, Telegram from Emma Carelli to Walter Mocchi, 7 October 1916.

[183] AVM, *AFVM*, b. H71, f. 9, Letter from Emma Carelli to Paolo Bruzzi, 1 September 1916.

[184] AVM, *AFVM*, b. H71, f. 9, Letter from Paolo Bruzzi to Walter Mocchi, Faustino Da Rosa, and Emma Carelli, 7 September 1916.

[185] I. Piazzoni, *Dal 'Teatro dei palchettisti' all'Ente autonomo*, p. 192.

[186] H. Sachs (ed.), *Nel mio cuore troppo d'assoluto: Le lettere di Arturo Toscanini* (Garzanti, 2003), p. 143.

citizenry. The obviously secretive arrival on the scene of Walter Mocchi – the most singular exponent of theatrical speculation – ... constitutes that violation .... Mr Walter Mocchi's arrival at La Scala is, therefore, a violation of [its] tradition and has sullied the steadfast purity of your management. It may also have prepared the way for a movie-house-like trash heap of performances put together in a hurry, as [happened] last season at the Teatro Colón .... This impresario has the impudence to write me that *he is creating, by agreement with you, Duke, a new technical mechanism for operating the theatre and that it ought to yield above-average artistic results, in his opinion.* I have already replied to him personally: 'No, Mr. Walter Mocchi, you cannot create anything, but only destroy everything – you cannot reform anything, but only deform everything – your theatrical career as a theatrical impresario demonstrates this .... Moving from one theatre to another, from one scandal to another, speculating one day on a singer's fame, the next on a composer, without ever doing anything that was artistically beautiful .... Duke Visconti di Modrone and Walter Mocchi – La Scala and the Colón of Buenos Aires – in other words, Patronage and Speculation ... Illegal couplings – not long-lasting, I hope.[']187

Toscanini's protest had no effect, and in the autumn of 1916 Mocchi and Visconti raised the stakes on the project through expanding it to include the two most important theatres in Paris, the Opéra and the Opéra Comique. This 'ingenious invention', as the Duke called Mocchi's idea,188 was the most ambitious plan that the impresario was to realize in his entire career.

After returning from the South American tour of La Teatral, Visconti went to serve his country in the war. He told La Scala's administrative director, Vittorio Mingardi, to go to Paris to meet with Mocchi. According to Mocchi, the strength of the French–Italian combination was

> not only the mere staging of French operas but also an exchange of productions to stage premieres in the original language, both in Italy and in France. Since the operas [in Italy, France and South America] will have their run in Italian according to our program, there are no costs for shipping [sets], the chorus or the orchestra. In fact, there will be another outlet for the Italian opera productions, which will be staged at L'Opera in Paris. Our only liabilities will be the payrolls of the French artists, which will have been previously set at war prices. And [the liabilities] will be compensated for [by means of] the payrolls of our artists moving to France .... We must also consider the increase of revenues given that will come from staging two premieres of each single opera in different languages, emphasizing the performances by L'Opera and Opéra Comique of Paris.189

---

187 H. Sachs, *Reflections on Toscanini* (Grove Weidenfeld, 1991), pp. 54–7.

188 AVM, *AFVM*, b. H71, f. 9, Telegram from Uberto Visconti di Modrone to Walter Mocchi [13–15 November 1916].

189 AVM, *AFVM*, b. H71, f. 9, Letter from Walter Mocchi to Paolo Bruzzi, 11 November 1916.

Figure 5.1 Walter Mocchi at about the time of Toscanini's protest
(*Il Teatro Illustrato*)

Political support for the project was crucial. Mocchi gained support from
both the Italian and the French governments and asked the Italian Ministry of
Fine Arts 'to cooperate with the support of the two governments'.[190] Official
government support for the project recused Visconti from any accusation of
speculation, such as the one Toscanini claimed in regard to the La Scala–Colón
agreement. However, the production of French-language productions at La
Scala seemed overly risky during difficult economic times. Visconti's attorney,
Paolo Bruzzi, stressed that 'giving the operas in the original language at the
Teatro alla Scala, which is the fulcrum of Italian opera, [wa]s not fully understood', and could be 'met by real hostility'.[191] Bruzzi's fears demonstrate how
the situation had worsened during the war, for in the past La Scala and Paris
enjoyed a close relationship and frequently exchanged productions. For example, the 'Saison Italienne' organized in the French capital by journalist-impre-
sario Gabriel Astruc in 1905 listed Uberto Visconti di Modrone as a 'Membre
du Comité de Patronage' (member of the patron committee)[192], and in 1908

---

[190] Ibid.
[191] AVM, *AFVM*, b. H71, f. 9, Letter from Paolo Bruzzi to Walter Mocchi, 2 November 1916.
[192] AVM, *AFVM*, b. I306, f. 1, Letter from Gabriel Astruc to Uberto Visconti di Modrone, 11 April
       1910.

Debussy's *Pelléas et Mélisande* was staged in Milan shortly after its debut at the Opéra Comique.

The contract creating the new combination of Costanzi, La Scala, Colón, L'Opera, and Opéra Comique was signed in Paris on 14 November 1916, by Jacques Rouché for L'Opéra, Pierre-Barthélemy Gheusi for the Opéra Comique, and Walter Mocchi, 'representing La Scala of Milan, the Costanzi of Rome, the enterprise Da Rosa – Mocchi granting the Colón of Buenos Aires and the Solís of Montevideo, and in his own name the Municipal Theatres of Rio de Janeiro and São Paulo'.[193] The convention was binding for 1917 and 1918, and its advantages were clearly stated in the first three articles of the agreement. Since the tight cooperation 'will allow the theatres of the Allied countries to increase the repertoire', the inter-oceanic network and the experience of the Italian impresarios in South America would guarantee the circulation of companies and artists in a theatrical market plagued by war. In a spirit of 'loyal and complete reciprocity', the plan came about

> through the desire to collaborate together, with the authorization of the French Government and under the patronage of their respective governments, to tighten the relationship between France and Italy, thus completing, through an artistic combination, the political and economic agreements that during and after the war must bind together the two countries.[194]

The partners promised to open

> the theatres of Paris and France not only to the authors but also to Italian artists. On the other hand, [the agreement aims to] open to French authors and artists not only Italian theatres but also all the major artistic centres of Spain, Portugal, South America, etc., that is, the markets in which Italy has exercised – and continues to exercise – almost exclusive influence.[195]

The agreement offered specifics concerning certain repertories and how the partnership would work. For example, La Scala, the Costanzi, and theatres in South America would perform 'operás comiques in French', and 'at least two unpublished lyriques françaises' would appear in Rome and Milan every year. To reciprocate, the two Parisian theatres promised 'to give during the two years 1917 and 1918 performances of Italian works in Italian, with Italian artists and conductors'. (Only one Italian production was required each year.) The reasons for these stipulations were aesthetic as well as practical:

---

[193] AVM, *AFVM*, b. H71, f. 9, Contract between Jacques Rouché, P. B. Gheusi, and Walter Mocchi, 14 November 1916.
[194] Ibid. [195] Ibid.

nothing is, from the artistic point of view, more appropriate to preserve the spirit and the character in which [a work] was conceived and created than to have it represented abroad, at least for the first time, in its original language by the artists who created it and under the direction of its author or a qualified conductor.[196]

Operation costs (orchestra, chorus, sets, and costumes) belonged to the individual theatres, which could 'exchange maquettes, sketches and set designs under conditions to be determined according to each case'.[197] The venues would share principal and secondary singers and conductors. It was also stated:

The management that imports the opera bears all the expenses of the show and keeps all its profits. It will refund the export fees to the management that exports the opera, i.e. artists' travel expenses, fees, transportation costs, etc. . . . New operas and rehearsals will both be refunded, the total of which will be established by mutual agreement once the program has been determined.[198]

The first season under the plan, 1916–1917, included productions that originated at the four European theatres and then circulated. Coming from L'Opéra and featuring its company and conductor, Vincent d'Indy's *Fervaal* played at La Scala while Camille Saint-Saëns's *Samson et Dalila* appeared at the Costanzi, conducted by the composer and also performed in French by L'Opéra's artists on 14 March 1917. The Opéra Comique provided Henri Rabaud's *Mârouf* and Xavier Leroux's *Cadeaux de Noël*, which played respectively in Rome and Milan. A production of Verdi's *Aida* from La Scala, sung in Italian with Italian singers and conductor, was followed with performances of the same work at the same theatre but now featuring 'French artists, in a French version'.[199] On 17 March 1917 the French version opened at Paris's L'Opéra.

La Scala's season, conducted by the Argentine maestro Hector Panizza, commenced with the rediscovery of Gaspare Spontini's *Fernando Cortez* on 26 December 1916, deemed 'an excellent artistic success' although the 'financial result did not correspond'.[200] The high-profile repertoire was supposed to include the Italian premiere of *Mârouf* as well as the world premiere of Mascagni's *Lodoletta*, but offstage drama kept these from happening at La Scala. The theatre's manager, Paolo Bruzzi, suggested to Mocchi that he should invest more promotional energy in Panizza, who was 'well viewed by the press . . ., and could be perfect for some advertisement', even though 'he is afraid that you don't think much of him'.[201] The relationship between Panizza and Mocchi was already strained and only intensified when the conductor refused to give the

---

[196] Ibid.   [197] Ibid.   [198] Ibid.   [199] Ibid.
[200] AVM, *AFVM*, b. H71, f. 9, Letter from Paolo Bruzzi to Walter Mocchi, 5 January 1917.
[201] Ibid.

podium to Rabaud for the Italian premiere of the Frenchman's *opéra comique*, *Mârouf*. Mocchi cancelled Panizza's contract, describing the incident as follows:

> What was asked of Maestro Panizza was purely and simply an act of artistic kindness towards Rabaud, and a simple execution of his agreement with the enterprise, since he was the general director of the performances – as Mascagni and Marinuzzi have been thousands of times – and he was obliged to give guidance and to prepare the runs that the composers would then conduct. Nobody asked him to rehearse the opera until the general rehearsal (and it would not have been extraordinary at all!), but simply to read or make someone read under his surveillance the opera with the orchestra to correct any mistakes in the parts .... According to Panizza's view, the theatres should stop having composers conduct their own operas .... I thank God this incident happened here, because I am now aware that I must not allow Maestro Panizza to work in America, where it is profitable for me to hire a lot of composers and conductors according to my taste, not to the taste of the cast.[202]

La Scala's management probably pressured Panizza to protest against the situation, since the theatre did not want to stage the 'very expensive production' from the Opéra Comique, particularly when wartime audiences were so small.[203] The debacle violated the agreement between La Scala and Opéra Comique, and Mocchi used this as the pretext to move the premiere of *Lodoletta* from La Scala to the Costanzi.[204] Gino Marinuzzi conducted *Lodoletta*'s debut at the Costanzi on 30 April 1917, and Mocchi subsequently hired him for the upcoming South American tour, during which *Lodoletta* was performed at the Colón with Enrico Caruso and Gilda Dalla Rizza.

Italian and French operas graced Mocchi's stages; German works were notably missing from the repertoire in the countries where Mocchi operated. Managers, including Mocchi, were wise not to program operas coming from countries with whom theirs were at war. Wagner's works, which had traditionally opened seasons at the Costanzi, were taken off schedules, as were older works by germanic composers, including Mozart. Emma Carelli explained this situation to the Municipality of Rome:

> I could have performed ... Mozart's *Don Giovanni*, for which I had also engaged Mr Battistini, but the recent demonstrations of the Roman audience against German music discouraged me from ... running such a risk. So, I replaced *Don Giovanni* with *Lucrezia Borgia*.[205]

[202] AVM, *AFVM*, b. H71, f. 9, Letter from Walter Mocchi to Paolo Bruzzi, 9 February 1917.

[203] AVM, *AFVM*, b. H71, f. 9, Letter of Paolo Bruzzi to Walter Mocchi, 5 January 1917.

[204] The negotiation was complicated, and it was correctly explained by Mascagni. See M. Morini, R. Iovino, and A. Paloscia (eds.), *Epistolario* ..., pp. 38–41.

[205] ASC, *X*, b. 56, f. 2, Letter from Emma Carelli to Valentino Leonardi, 2 December 1916.

The controversy over performing German works also existed in South America. In a letter to the Italian Embassy in Paris, the French Consulate in Buenos Aires related a tale of what transpired at the Colón when Mocchi asked a French singer to sing Wagner:

> During the most recent opera season at the Teatro Colón in Buenos Ayres [*sic*], which ended on the 12th of last month, an artist of the Paris Opera, engaged by the management of this theatre, was forced to sing a Wagner role, under penalty of termination of his contract. According to the information received by this Department, it seems that Mr. [Marcel] Journet did not ignore the obligations to which he should eventually be subject. And the management of the Beaux-Arts reserves the right to examine upon his return the extent to which his responsibility is hereby engaged. But what is important to note here is that, since Mr. Journet wished to avoid the clause of his contract concerning the performance of Wagner roles, he requested the intervention of our Minister of the Republic in Buenos Ayres [*sic*], and our representative appealed in vain to the good will and conciliatory spirit of the direction of the Theatre Colón. The Italian director of this theatre, Maestro Mocchi, would have [engaged him] especially for Wagner performances. Although the Minister of Foreign Affairs does not seem to exaggerate the incident, he also remarks how unfortunate it may seem that, in a neutral country, French and Italian artists lend their talent to the execution of works of art, whose performance, through an attitude of great expediency is not permitted elsewhere on stages in the Entente countries.[206]

It was not just German operas that suffered but also operettas, with their direct links to Vienna or Berlin. Although Mocchi 'allegedly publicly boasted that he would also recruit Austrian artists in order to earn money' and was accused of being a 'Germanophile',[207] in the summer of 1918 he replaced the usual Viennese operetta fare at the Costanzi with productions by Luigi Marazzi's Compagnia di operette Nazionale (National Operetta Company), which only performed operettas by Italian composers, including Carlo Lombardo's *La Regina del fonografo* (Queen of the Phonograph), *Madama di Tebe* and *La Signorina del Cinematografo* (The Young Lady of the Cinema), and Ruggero Leoncavallo's *La Vendemmia* (The Grape Harvest) and *Prestami tua moglie* (Lend Me Your Wife)).

Italian publishers, knowing the appeal the genre once held, had their main opera composers create shorter works in the lighter style to new libretti by successful authors. Among the works that appeared under this initiative were Puccini's *La Rondine* (The Swallow, 1917, libretto by Giuseppe Adami) and *Il*

---

[206] ACS, *CPC*, b. 3321, Letter from the Ministère des Affaires Etrangères to the Regia Ambasciata d'Italia a Parigi, Paris, 10 September 1917.

[207] ACS, *CPC*, b. 3321, Report to the Ministry of the Interior, Rome, 6 May 1918.

Trittico (The Triptych, 1918, especially the farce *Gianni Schicchi* with a libretto by Giovacchino Forzano) and Mascagni's postwar *Sì* (Yes, 1919, libretto by Carlo Lombardo, verses by Arturo Franci). 'What happened to the cheerful art of operetta?' asked the publisher Sonzogno during the launch of *Sì*.[208] 'Italian opera and operetta are a real ABC', but 'the audience considers them toys of little value, and the critics always ignore them unless they remember to talk badly'.[209]

While the war sidelined operetta *opéra comique* increased its international profile. After all, it was an *opéra comique*, *Mârouf*, that caused the row at La Scala, not an operetta. With the Opéra Comique in Paris as part of the collaborative agreement, the circulation of this repertoire onto foreign stages increased. Audiences in Italy and South America were now able to enjoy performances of Raoul Gunsbourg's *Le vieil aigle* (The Old Eagle), Xavier Leroux's *Cadeaux de Noël* (Christmas Presents), and older works such as Gounod's *Sapho* and Thomas's *Mignon*.

As the war drew to a close, the grand collaboration began to unravel. The French government suspended Mocchi's travel visa and accused the impresario of performing German operas in South America instead of replacing them with the allied French repertoire. The accusation was true, since Mocchi continued to stage Wagner and Viennese operettas in Argentina, Uruguay, and Brazil, where they remained in high demand. The South American theatrical market had become the cultural battleground between Italy and France. French managers formed their own rival coalition in opposition to Mocchi, as Emma Carelli explained:

> In Paris a [new] group was established by [Pierre-Barthélemy] Gheusi – manager of Opéra Comique – Lugné-Poe, [André] Messager, and even [Albert] Dalimier, former French secretary of the Beaux Arts and current impresario. These gentlemen formed a company with a half million capital, whose aim is the conquest of the South American market (including the Colón) through the expulsion of Italians .... They are supported by their government, which despite the alliance certainly produced a file against him ... in order to stop his boarding [on the liner] and to blow up the Italian lyrical season of the Colón, which is a 10 million francs business for Italy.[210]

Mocchi's French project, simply put, failed. To complicate matters, the situation in Italy was also changing. During the war, when the theatrical economy forced many theatres to close, singers themselves organized cooperatives to produce operas and sustain their livelihoods. The most successful and

---

[208] *L'Abicì*, 15 March 1920.   [209] Ibid.
[210] ACS, *CPC*, b. 3321, Letter from Emma Carelli to Vittorio Emanuele Orlando, Rome, 12 March 1918.

important of these 'cooperative' was the Società Italiana Fra gli Artisti Lirici (SIFAL), led by Italo Vicentini, Serse Peretti, and Mario Sammarco. Established in 1916, the association at one point boasted 600 members, and its board included such notables as Tito Ricordi, Renzo Sonzogno, Angelo Scandiani, and Tullio Serafin. In 1917 SIFAL took over the management of La Scala from Visconti, even though the decisive defeat of the Italian army at the Battle of Caporetto (24 October–19 November 1917) stopped all theatrical activity. SIFAL organized La Scala's lyrical season for autumn 1918,[211] which included works such as Verdi's *Aida*, Rossini's *Moses*, Boito's *Mefistofele*, Donizetti's *Don Pasquale*, and Riccardo Pick-Mangiagalli's *Il carillon magico* (The Magic Carillon). In 1919 the theatre morphed into an *ente autonomo* (autonomous body), and in 1920 it became state property. That same year SIFAL proposed a reform of the theatrical brokerage business 'to get rid of the sharking of the agencies'.[212] The company continued to hold an influential role under the fascist regime, and in 1923, at Mocchi's instigation, it organized the Congress for the Lyrical Theatre.

Meanwhile at the Costanzi, Carelli produced a season for 1918–1919 that she called 'the most complete that I have ever organized at the Costanzi'.[213] She underlined the profitability of the interoceanic trust: 'while La Scala in Milan, the Regio in Turin [and] the Carlo Felice in Genoa had to remain closed due to their struggles, the enterprise of the Costanzi won the same fights because of its connection with the main South American theatres'.[214] The conductors included Gino Marinuzzi, who conducted the premiere of his *Jacquerie*. Other offerings included a lavish production of *Don Carlo* and the Italian premiere of Puccini's *Il Trittico*, staged under the personal supervision of the composer. The season was enhanced through the work of the designers from La Scala, who had become a constant presence in Rome not only during the operetta seasons but also the operatic ones. The visual appeal of the productions definitely increased the Costanzi's reputation:

> A real improvement from the previous seasons has been the development of the scenery, that was a great part of the success of *Il Trittico*, *Rigoletto*, *Jacquerie*, *Aida* [and] *Bohème*, and which are true works of art by artists like Sala and Rovescalli. The exchange of sets between America and Italy has begun; and it allows the Costanzi – as the sole venue in Italy – to become a real 'repertoire theatre' that has nothing to envy from a great theatre such as the Metropolitan of New York or the Colón of Buenos Aires.[215]

---

[211] I. Piazzoni, *Dal 'Teatro dei palchettisti' all'Ente autonomo*, pp. 204–16.

[212] 'Contro i mediatori teatrali', *La Tribuna*, 1 January 1920.

[213] ASC, *X*, b. 56, f. 4, Letter from Emma Carelli to Valentino Leonardi, 26 April 1919.

[214] ASC, *X*, b. 56, f. 4, Letter from Emma Carelli to Rodolfo Lanciani, 4 August 1919.

[215] ASC, *X*, b. 56, f. 4, Letter from Emma Carelli to Valentino Leonardi, 26 April 1919.

World War I had a profound effect on Mocchi's transoceanic endeavours, most significantly through the addition of three world-class theatres – La Scala, L'Opéra, and the Opéra Comique – into his collaborative web. After the war, however, the theatres severed themselves from Mocchi's enterprise. Another theatrical crisis loomed in Italy, and coupled with the rise of the National Fascist Party, it was time for Mocchi to reinvent himself yet again.

6. New Initiatives, New Controversies: Mocchi in the 1920s and 1930s

Like most aspects of Italian society and culture, the theatre industry had to redefine itself after the war. Theatre manager Franco Liberati noted, 'The theatre is the thermometer of city life. When the halls are crowded, and the shows are staged with richness and luxury, that means that money can be spent . . . . Now the impresarios are afraid of risking their money because the audience no longer attends'.[216]

A large part of the reason why audiences stopped attending the theatre was the prohibitive cost of tickets. Massive inflation, a lack of public funding (due to the elimination of grants), and performers demanding higher salaries all contributed to the industry's fiscal challenges. In light of this, theatre managers were forced to raise ticket prices. Emma Carelli directly blamed inflation and the 'necessity of giving to artists and workers higher wages than they had before and during the war'[217] for the situation.

To reduce risk, lower costs, and still appeal to audiences, even with higher ticket prices, impresarios throughout Italy increased the number of familiar operas (ones that could guarantee a probable success) they produced and played them for relatively short runs. Works such as *La Bohème*, *Madama Butterfly*, *La Traviata, Rigoletto*, and *Il Trovatore* filled Italian stages, and a standard repertoire became ensconced, a situation that remains to the present day in opera houses worldwide.

Related to the ossification of repertoire, singers themselves posed additional challenges. More and more singers began to specialize in a limited number of roles, which they would perform in multiple theatres around the world. Earlier in the century this practice was of course normal for big international stars, but after the war singers who performed minor roles began to do the same. Foreign markets, where the pay was better, drew singers and conductors away from Italy, where inflation and a weak lira prevailed. Such factors made it

---

[216] 'I risultati del Congresso dei Lirici esposti alla "Stampa" da un competente', *La Stampa*, 17 March 1923.

[217] ASC, *X*, b. 56, f. 4, Letter from Adolfo Apolloni to the Prefect of Rome, 15 December 1919.

increasingly difficult for Italian impresarios to hire top-quality singers. Carlo Clausetti, director of Casa Ricordi, bemoaned the fact that the 'short contracts of the artists' had 'destroyed the lyrical companies, thus inevitably causing much less homogeneity and maturity of the staging' that often 'from one day to the next suffers a complete transformation'.[218]

Such problems affected the management of the theatres themselves. Municipalities and even the Italian government itself started to acquire opera houses, rather than provide grants for others to run them. The first theatre to be transformed into an *ente autonomo* (autonomous body) was the Teatro alla Scala in 1919. Then, on 4 May 1920 the 'Regio Decreto n. 567' imposed a 2 per cent tax on the revenues of spoken theatre and operetta performances (as well as cinema screening) in order to finance operas in the historic opera houses and thus provide for what the government called 'the artistic education of the people'. After a series of protests, the law was limited to the province of Milan as a means to finance the municipality-controlled Teatro alla Scala, its *ente autonomo*.

In 1923 the government established a grant of L. 200,000 'to increase the dramatic and lyrical arts'.[219] Operetta was excluded from the grant, because it was considered a mere commercial genre that could survive without any public funding. Another reason that operetta might have been disqualified was its role in a strike back in 1919 that closed all of Milan's theatres for fifty-six days. The protest started on 20 September 1919, when the orchestra players engaged by Suvini Zerboni's company at the Teatro dal Verme refused to accept the wage imposed by the company. The powerful SIFAL organization embraced the cause, and from this one operetta company the strike quickly spread to other genres and theatres, causing the first and to this day (2019) the longest shutdown of the performing arts in Italy. The protest became a huge sensation among the public,[220] and during the strike 'the theatrical world for the first time took up the arms of the political fight'.[221]

The power of the workers resulted in the creation of several new labour organizations. In 1920 the Confederazione Nazionale fra i Lavoratori del Teatro (National Confederation of Theatre Workers), inspired by socialist ideals, drew 13,700 members. To match the unionization of their employees, in 1922 the impresarios and the theatre owners formed the Corporazione Nazionale del Teatro (National Theatre Corporation). Walter Mocchi, of course, would find

---

[218] A. Gasco, 'Il Convegno di Roma per la crisi del teatro lirico', *Musica d'oggi*, April 1923.

[219] R. D. 15 July 1923, n. 1550.

[220] C. d'Ormeville, 'Fra S.O.M. e F.O.M.', *Gazzetta dei Teatri*, 9 October 1919.

[221] E. Scarpellini, *Organizzazione teatrale e politica del teatro nell'Italia fascista – nuova edizione riveduta e aggiornata* (LED, 2004), p. 102.

his place in these new arrangements, and in 1924 became the general secretary of the Sindacato degli Impresari (Union of the Impresarios), which he described as 'an entity that will aid in the solution of the operatic crisis' and as representing 'the beginning of a political, economic, and social organization that will define the fascist government'.[222]

Mocchi, at least publicly, was seen as a supporter of the Partito Nazionale Fascista (also known as the PNF or National Fascist Party) in Italy, which came to power in 1922, led by Benito Mussolini. As the impresario had done previously, he would use his political clout to benefit his savvy business interests.

Italian operetta, meanwhile, was floundering. Despite the wartime efforts of Ricordi and Sonzogno, fluctuating box-office results forced publishers to abandon the genre. The only Italian operetta that managed to capture audiences' attention during the postwar years was *Il paese dei campanelli* (The Country of the Bells, 1923, libretto by Carlo Lombardo, music by Lombardo and Virgilio Ranzato). Its success pushed Lombardo, its principal creator, to establish his own publishing company, which still holds copyrights for a large number of operettas today. Lombardo's hit, though, was an isolated case in a radically changing market.

The commercial exchange between Italy and South America slowed during the postwar period, which contributed to the further worsening of the Italian market. The decrease started during the war, largely because of the difficulties of travel, but South American theatres at the time wanted to create their own companies and repertories independent of the Europeans. This led to a period marked by the 'predominio de las compañias nacionales' (predominance of national companies), mostly in the spoken theatre.[223] Musical genres were profoundly affected. Already in 1910, during the centennial celebrations of the founding of the United Provinces of the Rio de la Plata, an anti-European opera movement promoted the creation in Argentina of a 'desired repertoire with identity value', inspired by a fictional rediscovery of 'real' South American music and legends.[224] The plan to continuously stage these new operas was never realized, and anti-opera sentiment continued throughout the decade so that by the early 1920s, members of the artistic elite were calling for a true refusal of European opera, 'whose disappearance from our musical activity would be a relief for the art and a freedom for the spirit.'[225]

---

[222] G. Marinuzzi, *Tema con variazioni. Epistolario artistico di un grande direttore d'orchestra* (Arnoldo Mondadori, 1995), p. 364.

[223] Seibel, *Historia del teatro argentino*, p. 542.

[224] A. E. Cetrangolo, *Dentro e fuori il teatro: Ventura degli italiani e del loro melodramma nel Rio de la Plata* (Cosmo Iannone, 2018), p. 185.

[225] G. O. Talamón, 'Coliseo', *Nosotros*, 148 (September 1921), p. 130.

Mocchi responded to this shift in taste in two ways. The first was through promoting operas by native-born composers in South American countries, and the second was by replacing the Italian and French artists and repertory with German ones.[226] In 1920 Mocchi received the grant to run the Municipal in São Paulo and promised 'a lyrical company expressly organized for Brazil' that could guarantee 'the independence of our theatre from Argentina' and fulfil 'the great development of the artistic taste of our audience' by avoiding 'the claimed inconvenience of bringing here tired companies at the end of their tour in the Southern capital cities'.[227] This was the beginning of an important association between Mocchi and Brazil. One of Mocchi's most important supporters in Brazil was the politician, musicologist, and composer Carlos de Campos (1866–1927). As the governor of São Paulo, de Campos gave Mocchi direct financial support, granted him a subsidy to manage the Municipal, and also organized fundraising campaigns to sustain the musical life of the main opera house. Perhaps to show his appreciation, Mocchi gave the premieres of two of de Campos's works at the Municipal, *A bela adormecida* (Sleeping Beauty, 1924) and *Um caso singular* (A Singular Case, 1926). Other Brazilian operas that Mocchi produced there included Carlos Gomes's *Salvador Rosa* and Alberto Nepomuceno's *Abul*. His seasons at the Municipal did not include operetta, not even de Campos's earlier *Um caso colonial* (A Colonial Case, 1902).[228] What did emerge at the Municipal, though, was a rediscovery of eighteenth-century Italian opera buffa. In 1926, Mocchi presented Cimarosa's *Il matrimonio segreto*, 'in the same production performed at the Costanzi', which was deemed 'a revival of great success'.[229] The main singer during these seasons was the Brazilian soprano Bidu Sayão (1902–1999), to whom we shall return later.

Along with managing the Municipal in São Paulo Mocchi maintained an active presence in Buenos Aires. In 1923, Mocchi and Faustino da Rosa again received the grant for the Colón. Controversy surrounded the decision, since their proposal was selected over a 'project of the Sociedad Nacional de Música, whose aim was to create an Argentine lyrical art under the direction of real and qualified Argentine artists, the only ones who have the right to realize this pursuit'.[230] To receive the grant, the impresario had to include several Argentine

---

[226] Mocchi did not completely abandon either repertoire. For example, in 1923 he contracted Charles Fontaine, a tenor at the Opéra Comique, to sing the French works that had made him famous (*Manon, Louise, Roméo et Juliette, Pélleas et Melisande, Ivan le Terrible*) in the main cities of Brazil and Argentina.

[227] *O Paiz*, 16 January 1920.

[228] The operetta was successfully staged for the first time in 1902 in São Paulo.

[229] 'A primeira novidade lyrica da companhia official', *Correio da Manhã*, 17 July 1926.

[230] G. O. Talamón, 'La licitación del teatro Colón', *Nosotros*, 151 (December 1921), p. 543. Among the twenty-seven artists that underwrote the proposal were Pascual de Rogatis (composer of *Huemac*), Carlos Pedrell (*Ardid de Amor*), Floro M. Ugarte (*Saika*), Felipe Boero

productions in the season, as well as work with the composer [Carlos] López Buchardo (1881–1948), president of the Asociación Wagneriana of Buenos Aires (Wagner Association of Buenos Aires). The association aimed to replace the most successful Italian and French repertoire with Wagner's *Musikdramas*, ideally performed in German. This connection with Buchardo became the impetus for Mocchi's promotion of German musical culture in South America and resulted in Mocchi creating Italian and German companies at the Colón.

Wanting to satisfy the cravings of the increasingly powerful German-speaking audience, in 1922 Mocchi brought the Vienna Philharmonic Orchestra,[231] conducted by Felix Weingartner, to perform a series of symphonic concerts and put on, for the first time in South America, performances of Wagner (*Der Ring des Nibelungen* and *Parsifal*) in the original language. This was not the first time the orchestra had toured South America, however. They had already done so in 1920, with Richard Strauss conducting, when 'the financial position of the Vienna State Opera was so bad' that they 'took the Vienna Philharmonic to South America to raise dollars'.[232] Mocchi's 1922 plan gave them a longer tour on a more solid financial footing than that they had experienced two years earlier.

The singers who performed Wagner came from several different German theatres. Konzertdirektion Daniel in Madrid contracted the principals, who included Helene Wildbrunn, Margarethe Jaeger-Weigert, and Carl Braun from the Berliner Staatsoper; Lotte Lehmann and Emil Schipper from the Wiener Staatsoper; and Walter Kirchhoff and Alice Mertens from the Wiener Volksoper. The stage director was Karl Wildbrunn, who one critic pointed out, 'could only prevent the worst. Unfortunately, our productions are still very far away from the European ones'.[233] The critics also noted that the choir of the Colón 'sang in Italian', but 'performed extraordinary things in *Parsifal*'.[234] (It was not uncommon at the time in many international productions of operas for the chorus and principals to sing in different languages.)

Despite some performance issues, noted above, the tour was a success. Critics praised Mocchi:

(*Tucuman y Arian y Dionisos*), Constantino Gaito (*Petronio*), and the conductors Ernesto Drangosch and Constantino Gaito.

[231] The Vienna Philharmonic Orchestra (Wiener Philharmoniker) is the orchestra of the Vienna State Opera (Wiener Staatsoper); it performs under the Philharmonic name for orchestral concerts. Hence, it would have been practical for the orchestra to perform both in concert and for opera performances.

[232] M. Kennedy, *Richard Strauss: Man, Musician, Enigma* (Cambridge University Press, 1999), p. 215.

[233] J. Franze, 'Die erste deutsche Oper in Buenos Aires', *Neue Zeitschrift für Musik*, 16 September 1922.

[234] Ibid.

> The German opera performances in Buenos Aires were a huge step forward. Walter Mocchi, the present impresario of the Colon Theatre, had taken the risk of breaking with the old established Italian operatic scheme and split South America's first theatre into German and Italian sections .... This was an enormous artistic and financial risk. Walter Mocchi deserves the credit of having organized the first stylish Wagner performances in South America. For the first time Wagner found some worthy interpreters, for the first time the 'Ring des Nibelungen' and 'Parsifal', freed from all the bells of the Italian tradition, performed in the original language; for the first time Wagner was heard inwardly .... Wagner performances in German represented the fulfilment of a long-held wish of a significant number of Argentine intellectuals. The audience went along splendidly with the first performance of 'Parsifal', which opened the season, and remained faithful to the German opera season.[235]

Mocchi's 1922 tour started to change a performing tradition in Argentina. 'Wagner is always sung in Italian, without any sentiment for the huge monumentality of his powerful gesture and style', protested the main critic from the German community in Buenos Aires before the Vienna Philharmonic tour was announced: 'Musikdramas become melodramas. That fulfils the taste of the audience, which wants to enjoy the singer in the first place and has no interest in the deepest ideas of the scenic action.'[236]

Most who attended the Colón in 1922, though, were not fans of Wagner and did not appreciate the change in repertoire. As was mentioned in a local newspaper:

> The Municipality must not forget that the Colón Theatre is open to all and not only to the partners of the Wagneriana, and that it has already been proven that thousands of citizens of this huge and cosmopolitan city prefer to delight in *Il Trovatore* sung by Martinelli or *La Bohème* by Claudia Muzio, or in *La copa del olvido*, cried by any national divo of 'cabaret'.[237]

So, to please the majority of their audience, Mocchi and Da Rosa planned a fine season of Italian opera and re-engaged Pietro Mascagni as conductor and composer. Mascagni once again proved a popular draw, which was necessary, since, as reported when a small group of elites were demanding the Wagner performances at the Colón:

> The huge cost of the seasons [is] sustained by the support from a small class of rich people, [but it has to fulfil] the eclectic taste of the public, with traditional inclinations – which is not as reprehensible as it is said to be – towards the Italian opera and the great singers ... unless the Municipality is willing to invest millions of Pesos.[238]

---

[235] Ibid.

[236] J. Franze, 'Konzert – und Oper – Verhältnisse in Buenos Aires', *Neue Zeitschrift für Musik*, 16 September 1921.

[237] R. F. Giusti, 'La licitación del Colón', *Nosotros*, 152 (January 1922), pp. 103–4.   [238] Ibid.

As explained by the impresario, the double presence of the Italian and the German companies should 'realize the miracle of harmony and homogeneity not only from the artistic point of view', but also 'the sincere rapprochement of the artists of Italy and Germany' after the war.[239] Conflicts did remain, however. For example, when Mascagni conducted the South American premiere of his opera *Il piccolo Marat* (Little Marat) at the Colón, the success of Weingartner and the Vienna Philharmonic overshadowed it. This incident was indicative of what would become a major criticism of Mocchi: he invested more in German artists than in Italian ones. Even in Italy, Mocchi engaged the German conductor Otto Klemperer to lead the 1922–1923 season at the Costanzi.

Following the success of the 1922 Vienna Philharmonic tour, Mocchi (see Figure 6.1) arranged another tour for the venerable orchestra the next year, this time with Richard Strauss conducting. The tour included *Salome* (performed on 18 October 1923) and ended up losing a lot of money, for, as one critic noted, although 'a very remarkable success, … the company played many times in front of an empty theatre'.[240]

The shift to German operas also affected operetta. As early as 1910, German operetta troupes were starting to replace Italian ones in South America.[241] In 1921 Mocchi brought a German operetta troupe[242] to the Coliseo in Buenos Aires for a respectable run:

> The German operetta, which performed here from 21 April to 12 June, had great success with works by Kallman [*sic*], Lehar, Leo Fall, Goetze, Jessel. The performance of *Die Fledermaus* did not fulfil all expectations, but the staging of Kuennecke's *Wenn Liebe erwacht* was a veritable delight.[243]

German operettas were delighting audiences in South America at the expense of Italian works.[244] Mascagni, among others, was greatly concerned about Mocchi turning away from Italian interests towards German ones. The influential composer discussed the matter privately with Benito Mussolini, head of the fascist government, at the Palazzo Chigi on 26 January 1923.[245] Mocchi, as an expert former politician, managed to turn what had started as a personal disagreement into a large-scale public debate in the national press regarding

---

[239] *Comoedia*, 19 June 1922.

[240] J. Soler Vilardero, 'Argentine', *Le Ménestrel*, 19 October 1923.

[241] A. Philipp, 'Aus Südbrasilien', *Neue Zeitschrift für Musik*, 5 August 1922.

[242] The name of the company remains unknown. It was advertised simply as a 'German operetta company'.

[243] J. Franze, 'Konzert – und Oper – Verhältnisse in Buenos Aires', *Neue Zeitschrift für Musik*, 16 September 1921.

[244] This trend did not last long, for operetta companies started to fail, such as Leo Fall's in 1925.

[245] 'Mascagni espone all'on. Mussolini le sue amare esperienze d'America', *La Stampa*, 27 January 1923.

Figure 6.1 Walter Mocchi in the 1920s

the general crisis of theatre at a time of tremendous change. As a result of heated exchanges, two congresses were organized, the Congress of the Lyrical Art, held in Rome on 15 March 1923, and the Congress for the Dramatic and Operetta Theatre, held in Milan on 15 January 1924.[246] Inspired by Mocchi, SIFAL and the fascist government planned the 1923 congress, the most important result of which was a general acknowledgement 'that the theatrical crisis [wa]s a partial aspect of a more general crisis, because it [wa]s both an economic and a cultural crisis'.[247] Heated arguments about the opera world took place, and, in a scene that could have appeared in a verismo opera, Mocchi slapped Mascagni during a debate, resulting in a fist fight and a challenge to a duel.[248] Beyond these theatrical aspects, the Congress developed a document concerning the creation of *enti autonomi* for the management and financing of opera houses that was discussed in parliament, codifying what had happened at La Scala in 1919. The Congress's success prompted the organization of another conference the next year.

The 1924 congress included debates on the public funding of spoken theatre, variety theatre, and operetta, as well as procedures for contracts and management. Both congresses pushed the fascist government to consider the theatrical system as a whole, and many of the resolutions eventually became law.

---

[246] The event was organized by the Corporazione Nazionale del Teatro, Società Italiana degli Autori, and Associazione fra Proprietari ed Esercenti di Teatri. The debate focused on management and legal matters, not aesthetic issues. 'Il Congresso Nazionale del Teatro di prosa e operettistico', *Il Popolo d'Italia*, 16 January 1924.

[247] 'I voti del Congresso per il Teatro lirico', *Il Popolo d'Italia*, 16 March 1923.

[248] 'Mascagni manda i padrini a Walter Mocchi', *La Stampa*, 16 March 1923. The issue was solved privately the next day ('Il verbale di conciliazione circa la vertenza Mascagni-Mocchi', *La Stampa*, 17 March 1923).

By the mid-1920s, the South American transatlantic marketplace was showing signs of collapse. Despite the critical and popular success of the 1923 season at the Solís in Montevideo, Uruguay, conducted by Gino Marinuzzi, the financial crisis in neighbouring Argentina cost 'the enterprise a huge loss of money'.[249] The cooperative seasons organized by Charles Séguin between Buenos Aires and Montevideo also failed, but the biggest catastrophe was the tour of the Grand-Guignol Paris, which 'had success in terms of respect, but the financial result was void'.[250] Mocchi wrote to Marinuzzi:

> you do not get the meaning of the huge financial disaster of the current season: it had been one of the best in my entrepreneurial career, but its failure confirmed the financial and theatrical crisis that menaces the existence of Lyrical Theatre in South America.[251]

The collapse of Mocchi's South American activities had a devastating impact on the Costanzi. With all the problems in Italy, Mocchi and Carelli had been using profits from the South American ventures to cover liabilities at the Costanzi. The couple, as majority shareholders of the STIN, used the corporation as a means to obtain loans and defer bills. They eventually had to mortgage the company's sole asset, the Costanzi itself, and in January 1924, the couple legally separated. The situation worsened, and in late 1925 Mocchi and Carelli had to sell their majority shares in the STIN to the fascist governor of Rome. On 18 May 1926, the regime purchased 376 shares of the company at the inflated price of L. 11.906.662, covering Mocchi and Carelli's losses.[252] The sale also gave the capital city its desired Royal Opera House.[253] The couple was excluded from running the theatre, and the intense stress of the situation caused them to go their separate ways.

Carelli aimed at becoming artistic director at the Teatro San Carlo in Naples. When this hope was dashed, she fell into depression and tragically died while driving her red Lancia Lambda sports car. A few days before the accident that took her life, she wrote to a friend: 'Three passions I had in my life: Walter Mocchi, the Costanzi, and this damned car, which one day will crush me!'[254]

Mocchi, by contrast, managed to reinvent his life once again. In 1925 he moved to São Paulo, Brazil, where he tightened his political connections and

---

[249] J. Soler Vilardero, 'Argentine', *Le Ménestrel*, 19 October 1923.

[250] J. Soler Vilardero, 'Uruguay', *Le Ménestrel*, 19 October 1923.

[251] G. Marinuzzi, *Tema con variazioni:Epistolario artistico di un grande direttore d'orchestra* (Arnoldo Mondadori, 1995), p. 335.

[252] The couple earned L. 1.886.662 in cash: the difference was used to cover the STIN's liabilities. ASC, *STIN – Appendice*, b. 1, f. 2, *Dal Verbale delle Deliberazioni del Governatore adottate il giorno 18 maggio 1926 – Acquisto delle azioni del Teatro Costanzi*.

[253] The official architect for the regime, Marcello Piacentini, had already planned the refurbishment of the Costanzi in 1923. The Teatro Reale dell'Opera di Roma opened in 1928.

[254] A. Carelli, *Emma Carelli: trent'anni di vita del teatro lirico* (Maglione, 1932), p. 317.

'threw himself into Benito's arms, becoming a fierce and convinced fascist'.[255] Supported by the founder of the local 'Fascio', Emidio Rocchetti, and his old friend de Campos, now the powerful president of the federal state, Mocchi resumed his role as one of the most powerful impresarios in South America. After Carelli's tragic death, Mocchi married Bidu Sayão, the principal soprano at the Municipal in São Paolo, and managed her highly successful opera career, which included critically acclaimed performances throughout Brazil and at La Scala, San Carlo, the Costanzi, and the Metropolitan Opera.

To support his entrepreneurial activity, Mocchi established yet another company, the Società Teatrale Italo-Brasiliana (also known as 'Empreza Theatral Italo-Brasileira'), with a capital investment of 100,000 reais. Despite its name, the company's activity was limited to Brazil. It received annual funding from the city of São Paulo to continue activities at the Municipal and a grant from Rio de Janeiro to run its Teatro Municipal. Mocchi's presence in Brazil caused a great deal of vexation, partly because of his main patron, the controversial de Campos,[256] and partly because the Brazilian elite considered the businessman to be 'a limiting factor to the flourishing of composers, artists and a national opera project'.[257] The intelligentsia as a whole, however, did not really care about what happened at the opera house. As one critic noted during the run of de Campos's *A Bela adormecida*:

> The so-called elite public, out of snobbery, only goes to the 'premieres' at the Municipal, and never for the sake of Art . . . [T]hese chic people will not even deign to go to the most luxurious theatre of the artistic capital of the country for the first performance of a lyrical opera by a Brazilian author, performed by a group of the most prestigious national artists . . . High society prefers to see Carlito on the screen in a cinema or to dance exotic dances in the elegant dance halls.[258]

During the 1930s Mocchi continued to secure public funds for his theatres on both sides of the Atlantic, which now were operating independently rather than through a network. In Italy, he held the grant to operate the Teatro San Carlo in Naples (the same theatre Carelli had hoped to lead) from 1932 to 1934. This was done with the support of the fascist regime and through Mocchi's new artist management company, Artisti Lirici Associati (Associated Opera Artists).[259] In the autumn of 1933 he entered into an agreement with the Ente Italiano

---

[255] 'Le gesta dei fascisti in Brasile. Walter Mocchi, oratore del fascio di S. Paolo', *La Difesa*, 19 May 1927.

[256] A good summary can be found in 'Uno scandalo alle viste?', *Il Pasquino Coloniale*, 21 May 1927.

[257] J. M. Coli, 'O negócio da arte: as influências da gestão e organização italiana na ópera lírica em São Paulo', *Opus*, 22 (2016), 173.

[258] '"A Bela adormecida" no Municipal', *Vida Moderna*, 9 May 1924.

[259] F. Mancini, *Il Teatro di San Carlo 1737–1987* (Electa, 1987), vol. I, p. 175.

Audizioni Radiofoniche (Body of Italian Radio Broadcasting, EIAR) to plan the opera seasons at the Teatro Argentina in Rome. Meanwhile in Brazil he established the still-operating Associação Brasileira de Artistas Líricos (Association of Brazilian Opera Artists) in 1932. The Italian and the Brazilian companies had no relationship.

Mocchi maintained a public image of supporting the fascist regime, something that was essential in order for him to continue to operate his multinational businesses, and even worked as an informant for the fascist secret service (OVRA). Glimpses of his true thoughts, however, exist in several recently discovered documents. In 1936 the fascists accused Mocchi's former political ally, the socialist Arturo Labriola, of not fully supporting the regime. Mocchi reminded his friend of their revolutionary years and advised him on how to deal with the fascists. The letter was intercepted by the secret police.

> The regime is constructed like a piece of granite: it has created a mentality of its own, a style, a language. Italy is like a new country whose shores are very far away for those who return today from democratic and liberal countries. Moreover, it is filled with new officials ... who allow you to freely express the most daring ideas in the matter of expropriations, provided that you do not pronounce the word 'socialism', which is taboo ....[260]

There were no consequences for Mocchi after the letter was intercepted. Furthermore, after the arrest of Benito Mussolini on 25 July 1943, a police report described Mocchi as:

> the shady Vatican figure who routinely stays at the Plaza .... At the hotel he is well known as anti-fascist and former pederast. Since 25 July he looks very happy and is more talkative .... He doesn't miss any occasion to celebrate the fall of fascism and display his joy.[261]

After the defeat of fascism in 1943, Mocchi returned permanently to Brazil. No longer was he crossing the Atlantic managing an interoceanic business empire. His multiple business ventures had dissolved, and from 1948 until his death in 1955 Mocchi worked for the Artistic Committee of the Municipality of Rio de Janeiro. The musical and theatrical impresario whose very name had inspired a mixture of curiosity, hatred, fear, respect, and envy on an international scale spent his final years employed as a civil servant far away from his homeland.

---

[260] ACS, *WM*, Letter from Walter Mocchi to Arturo Labriola, 28 March 1936.

[261] ACS, *WM*, Informativa, 23 August 1943. This was the first time Mocchi was accused of pederasty. The accusation might be related to his attempt to find support from the Vatican. It must also be noted that these kinds of allegations and accusations were very common in police reports of the time.

Epilogue

Walter Mocchi was a forward-looking, controversial, entrepreneurial, clever, sharp-witted, and ruthless impresario who created and managed a transoceanic theatrical empire in the first third of the twentieth century. When Italy found itself in various theatrical crises, Mocchi used his business acumen and artistic foresight to craft viable solutions, including westward expansion to South America.

Mocchi's various enterprises – which included the Sociedad Teatral Ítalo-Argentina (the STIA), the Società Teatrale Internazionale (the STIN), La Teatral, the Agenzia Teatrale Italo-Sud-Americana, and an expanded network during World War I that included not only the theatres under La Teatral but also La Scala, L'Opéra and the Opéra Comique, and the Società Teatrale Italo-Brasiliana – reflected an individual who realized that the theatrical world was in constant flux and that its business side needed to be able to adjust accordingly and quickly to shifting dynamics in the arts industry. While his efforts were most visible in the sphere of opera, he played an extremely significant role in the promotion and circulation of more popular forms of musical theatre, namely operetta and *opéra comique*, on both sides of the Atlantic.

Although the circulation of large-scale productions was nothing new, the way Mocchi did it on a large transatlantic scale was indeed revolutionary. He offered an early example of what Stephen Greenblatt calls 'cultural mobility', namely the 'urgent need to rethink fundamental assumptions about the fate of culture in an age of global mobility'.[1] Mocchi not only brought European musical theatre forms to South America but also supported the global importance of South American cities in terms of opera by staging world premieres of works by Italian superstars in Buenos Aires (e.g. Mascagni's *Isabeau*) and by producing titles by Brazilian composers in São Paolo. The Costanzi–Colón connection was especially important in promoting this idea, whereby audiences in Buenos Aires could hear the same orchestra and chorus conducted by the same conductor and with the same principals who had recently performed the same work in Rome.

Mocchi's tightly coordinated system of theatres and companies also offers an early example of the corporate practice of 'vertical integration', which *Strategic Management Insight* defines as

> a strategy used by a company to gain control over its suppliers or distributors in order to increase the firm's power in the marketplace, reduce transaction costs and secure supplies or distribution channels.[2]

---

[1] S. Greenblatt, 'Cultural Mobility: an Introduction', in Stephen Greenblatt (ed.), *Cultural Mobility: A Manifesto* (Cambridge University Press, 2010), pp. 1–2.

[2] Ovidijus Jurevicius, 'Vertical Integration', *Strategic Management Insight*, 13 April 2013, www .strategicmanagementinsight.com/topics/vertical-integration.html (accessed 20 July 2019).

By creating umbrella organizations that controlled theatres, productions (including sets and costumes), companies (including orchestras, choruses, and dancers), principals, and even conductors, Mocchi realized the potential for vertical integration in the theatre industry. He strengthened his business position through (sometimes underhanded) agreements with civic officials and music publishers. He envisioned, and in many ways created, a holistic theatrical ecosystem in terms of performance and production. This approach extended to the types of works he featured on stage. Operas in multiple languages (Italian, French, German), spoken dramas, and of course operettas constituted nodes in his symbiotic network of theatrical genres.

Mocchi also realized that it was crucial to the survival of any performing arts entity that it offers a variety of repertoire to appeal to different audiences. Operas would generally lose money and lighter fare, such as operetta, could attract huge audiences and offset the losses incurred by expensive operas. Many opera companies nowadays, perhaps unknowingly, follow Mocchi's model when they include a popular work on the season, perhaps a musical, to draw new and large audiences to the opera house.

If the stories of Walter Mocchi and Emma Carelli seem the stuff of which movies are made, a film based on their lives and careers, *La Prima Donna*, starring Licia Maglietta and directed by Tony Saccucci, does just that. The biopic's premiere on 14 October 2019 took place at Rome's Teatro dell'Opera, the house that long ago was known as the Costanzi. How appropriate for Carelli to be honoured in the very venue whose reputation she helped create.

As studies of musical theatre, including operetta and opera, expand to include producers, modes of circulation, and the business side of the genre, Mocchi's endeavours and legacy demonstrate how one individual, a 'Buffalo Bill' individualist of sorts, could identify new opportunities in South America, create and manage an extensive network of organizations to meet those needs, and institute a specific type of cultural mobility – albeit one infused with problematic aspects of economic and material colonialism – that remains to the present day.

Abbreviations

ACS	Archivio Centrale dello Stato, Rome
CPC	*Casellario Politico Centrale, 1897–1929*
WM	*Ministero dell'Interno. Divisione generale di pubblica sicurezza. Divisione Polizia politica. Fascicoli personali, Walter Mocchi*
ASC	Archivio Storico Capitolino, Rome
STIN	*Società Teatrale Internazionale*
X	*Ripartizione X (Antichità e Belle Arti) 1907–1920*
ASCC	Archivio Storico della Camera di Commercio di Roma
TCP	*Fondo Ex Tribunale Civile e Penale di Roma – Sezione Commerciale*
AVM	Archivio Visconti di Modrone, Università Cattolica del Sacro Cuore – Dipartimento di Storia dell'economia, della società e di scienze del territorio 'Mario Romani', Milan
AFVM	*Archivio della Famiglia Visconti di Modrone – Serie proprie ad personam*

References

Sources

This research draws upon a significant number of hitherto unexplored sources, most significantly the STIN company archive held at the Archivio Storico Capitolino in Rome. This repository is considered one of the largest private theatrical archives in Italy (41 boxes, 422 folders, 5.5 metres in length).[1] Besides accounting records, the archive contains correspondence and other written documents.[2] Other repositories consulted for the study include the archives of the Camere di Commercio (Boards of Trade) in Rome and Milan, the Archive Visconti di Modrone in Milan, and the Municipal Archives of Rome, Genoa, Parma, Turin, and Buenos Aires.

Newspapers and Magazines (Consulted Periods in Parentheses)

Avanti! (1905–1931), Milan

L'Arte Drammatica (1905–1922), Milan

Ars et Labor (1907–1921), Milan

Boletin Oficial de la República Argentina (1907–1930), Buenos Aires

Caras y caretas (1898–1941), Buenos Aires

Correio da Manhã (1907–1955), Rio de Janeiro

Correio Paulistano (1905–1955), São Paulo

Corriere della Sera (1903–1931), Milan

Comœdia (1907–1914), Paris

Giornale d'Italia (1907–1926), Rome

Gazzetta dei Teatri (1908–1924), Milan

Le Ménestrel (1920–1925), Paris

Die Musik (1920–1925), Berlin and Leipzig

La Nación (1907–1925), Buenos Aires

Neue Zeitschrift für Musik (1920–1924), Leipzig

Nosotros (1921–1922), Buenos Aires

O Paiz (1907–1929), Rio de Janeiro

Il Popolo d'Italia (1923), Milan

La Revista Artística de Buenos Aires (1907–1908)

---

[1] M. Paoletti, G. Ludovisi, and M. T. De Nigris, *La Società teatrale internazionale 1908–1931: archivio e storia di una grande impresa teatrale* (Viella, 2016).

[2] M. Paoletti, *Mascagni, Mocchi, Sonzogno* …

La Stampa (1904–1931), Turin
Il Teatro illustrato (1907–1914), Milan
Il Tirso (1908–1910), Rome
La Tribuna (1908–1925), Rome

Select Bibliography

Baia Curioni, S. *Mercanti dell'Opera: Storie di Casa Ricordi* (Il Saggiatore, 2011)

Balme, C. 'The Bandmann Circuit: Theatrical Networks in the First Age of Globalization', *Theatre Research International*, 40 (2015), 19–36

Balme, C.'Maurice E. Bandmann and the Beginnings of a Global Theatre Trade', *Journal of Global Theatre History*, 1 (2016), 34–45

Barone, G. 'La modernizzazione italiana dalla crisi allo sviluppo', in G. Sabbatucci and V. Vidotto (eds.), *Storia d'Italia* (Rome-Bari: Laterza, 1995), vol. III, pp. 256–370

Bastos, S. *Carteira do Artista: Apontamentos para a Historia do Theatro Portuguez e Brazileiro* (Bertrand, 1898)

Becker, T. 'Globalizing Operetta before the First World War', *Opera Quarterly*, 33 (2017), 7–27

Benzecry, C. E. 'An Opera House for the "Paris of South America": Pathways to the Institutionalization of High Culture', *Theory and Society*, 43 (2014), 169–96

Branchard, A. *Comment on organise une tournée mondiale* (Stock, 1913)

Caamaño,R. *La historia del Teatro Colón 1908–1968* (Cinetea, 1969)

Carelli, A. *Emma Carelli: trent'anni di vita del teatro lirico* (Maglione, 1932)

Cavaglieri, L. *Trust teatrali e diritto d'autore (1894–1910): La tentazione del monopolio* (Titivillus, 2012)

Cetrangolo, A. E. *Ópera, barcos y banderas: El melodrama y la migración en Argentina (1880–1920)* (Biblioteca Nueva, 2015)

Cetrangolo, A. E. and M. Paoletti (eds.), *I fiumi che cantano. L'opera italiana nel bacino del Rio de la Plata* (Alma Mater Studiorum Bologna, 2020)

Cimmino, A. 'Walter Mocchi', in *Dizionario Biografico degli Italiani* (Istituto dell'Enciclopedia italiana, 1960), vol. 75 (2011)

Coli, J. M. 'O negócio da arte: as influências da gestão e organização italiana na ópera lírica em São Paulo', *Opus*, 22 (2016)

Crespi Morbio,V. (ed.), *Caramba: mago del costume* (Amici della Scala, 2008)

Cymbron, L. 'Camões in Brazil: Operetta and Portuguese Culture in Rio de Janeiro, circa 1880', *Opera Quarterly*, 30 (2014), 330–361.

Degrada, F. 'Il segno e il suono: Storia di un editore musicale e del suo mondo', in *Musica, musicisti, editoria: 175 anni di Casa Ricordi, 1808–1983* (Ricordi, 1983)

Devoto, F. J. *Historia de la inmigración en la Argentina* (Editorial Sudamericana, 2003)

Devoto, F. J. *Storia degli italiani in Argentina* (Donzelli, 2007)

Forgacs, D. and S. Gundle. *Mass Culture and Italian Society from Fascism to the Cold War* (Indiana University Press, 2008)

Frajese, V. *Dal Costanzi all'Opera: cronache, recensioni e documenti in 4 volumi* (Capitolium, 1977)

Gentile, E. 'L'emigrazione italiana in Argentina nella politica di espansione del nazionalismo e del Fascismo', *Storia contemporanea*, 3 (1986), 355–96

Gheusi, P. B. *Guerre et Théâtre* (Berger-Levrault, 1919)

Greenblatt, S. 'Cultural Mobility: An Introduction', in S. Greenblatt (ed.), *Cultural Mobility: A Manifesto* (Cambridge University Press, 2010)

Leonhardt, N. *Theater über Ozeane: Vermittler transatlantischen Austauschs (1890–1925)* (Vandenhoeck & Ruprecht, 2018)

Lugné-Poe. *La Parade: Sous les etoiles. Souvenirs de théâtre (1902–1912)* (Gallimard, 1933)

Mancini, F. *Il Teatro di San Carlo 1737–1987* (Electa, 1987)

Marinuzzi, G. *Tema con variazioni: Epistolario artistico di un grande direttore d'orchestra* (Arnoldo Mondadori, 1995)

McCleary, K. 'Popular Theater in Buenos Aires: The Madrid of South America?', *The Metropole*, 16 May 2018, Urban History Association, https://themetropole .blog/2018/05/16/popular-theater-in-buenos-aires-the-madrid-of-south-america (accessed 4 October 2019)

Mocchi, W. *I moti italiani del 1898: lo stato d'assedio a Napoli e le sue conseguenze* (Enrico Muca, 1901)

Morini, M., R. Iovino, and A. Paloscia (eds.), *Epistolario* (Libreria Musicale Italiana, 1996)

Morini, M. and P. Ostali, Jr. (eds.), *Casa Musicale Sonzogno: Cronologie, saggi, testimonianze* (Sonzogno, 1995)

Nicolodi, F. 'Il teatro lirico e il suo pubblico', in S. Soldani and G. Turi (eds.), *Fare gli italiani* (Il Mulino, 1993), vol. I, pp. 257–339

Nugnes, P., and S. Massimini. *Storia dell'Operetta* (Ricordi, 1984)

Orselli, C. *Pietro Mascagni* (L'Epos, 2011)

Paoletti, M. *Mascagni, Mocchi, Sonzogno. La Società Teatrale Internazionale (1908–1931) e i suoi protagonisti* (Alma Mater Studiorum Bologna, 2015), https://doi.org/10.6092/unibo/amsacta/4235.

Paoletti, M. 'La red de empresarios europeos en Buenos Aires (1880–1925). Algunas consideraciones preliminares', *Revista Argentina de Musicología*, 21 (2020), 51–76

Pellettieri, O. (ed.) *Inmigración italiana y teatro argentino* (Galerna, 1999)

Piazzoni, I. *Dal "Teatro dei palchettisti" all'Ente autonomo: la Scala, 1897–1920* (La Nuova Italia, 1995)

Piazzoni, I. 'Il governo e la politica per il teatro: tra promozione e censura (1882–1900)', in C. Sorba (ed.), *L'Italia fin de siècle a teatro* (Carocci, 2004)

Rebellato, D. *Theatre and Globalization* (Palgrave Macmillan, 2009)

Rosmini, E. *Legislazione e giurisprudenza dei teatri* (Hoepli, 1893)

Rosselli, J. 'Latin America and Italian Opera: A Process of Interaction, 1810–1930', *Revista de musicologia, 16* (1993), 139–45

Rosselli, J. 'The Opera Business and the Italian Immigrant Community in Latin America 1820–1930: The Example of Buenos Aires', *Past & Present*, 127 (1990), 155–82

Ruffo, T. *La mia parabola: Memorie* (Staderini, 1977)

Scarpellini, E. *Organizzazione teatrale e politica del teatro nell'Italia fascista – nuova edizione riveduta e aggiornata* (LED, 2004)

Seibel, B. *Historia del teatro argentino: Desde los rituales hasta 1930* (Corregidor, 2002)

Severi, S. *I teatri di Roma* (Newton Compton, 1989)

Sorba, C. 'The Origins of the Entertainment Industry: The Operetta in Late Nineteenth-Century Italy', *Journal of Modern Italian Studies*, 2 (2006), 282–302

Sorba, C. 'To Please the Public: Composers and Audiences in Nineteenth-Century Italy', *Journal of Interdisciplinary History*, 36 (2006), 595–614

Szwarcer, C. *Teatro Maipo: 100 años de historia entre bambalinas* (Corregidor, 2010)

Weber, J. I., L. Martinovich, and P. Camerata. 'Itinerari di compagnie liriche italiane attraverso le città del litorale fluviale argentino (1908–1910)', in A. E. Cetrangolo and M. Paoletti (eds.), *I fiumi che cantano. L'opera italiana nel bacino del Rio de la Plata* (Alma Mater Studiorum Bologna, 2020)

Wolkowicz, V. 'En busca de la identidad perdida: los escritos de Gastón Talamón sobre música académica de y en Argentina en la revista Nosotros (1915–1934)', in V. Eli Rodríguez and E. Torres Clemente (eds.), *Música y construcción de identidades: poéticas, diálogos y utopías en Latinoamérica y España* (Sociedad Española de Musicología, 2018), 33–44

Cambridge Elements ☰

Musical Theatre

William A. Everett

University of Missouri-Kansas City

William A. Everett, PhD is Curators' Distinguished Professor of Musicology at the University of Missouri-Kansas City Conservatory, where he teaches courses ranging from medieval music to contemporary musical theatre. His publications include monographs on operetta composers Sigmund Romberg and Rudolf Friml and a history of the Kansas City Philharmonic Orchestra. He is contributing co-editor of the *Cambridge Companion to the Musical* and the *Palgrave Handbook of Musical Theatre Producers*. Current research topics include race, ethnicity and the musical and London musical theatre during the 1890s.

About the Series

Elements in Musical Theatre focus on either some sort of 'journey' and its resulting dialogue, or on theoretical issues. Since many musicals follow a quest model (a character goes in search of something), the idea of a journey aligns closely to a core narrative in musical theatre. Journeys can be, for example, geographic (across bodies of water or land masses), temporal (setting musicals in a different time period than the time of its creation), generic (from one genre to another), or personal (characters in search of some sort of fulfilment). Theoretical issues may include topics relevant to the emerging scholarship on musical theatre from a global perspective and can address social, cultural, analytical, and aesthetic perspectives.

Cambridge Elements ≡

Musical Theatre

Elements in the Series

A Huge Revolution of Theatrical Commerce: Walter Mocchi
and the Italian Musical Theatre Business in South America
Matteo Paoletti

A full series listing is available at: www.cambridge.org/EIMT

Lightning Source UK Ltd.
Milton Keynes UK
UKHW021958050820
367772UK00009B/103